RETHINKING
GEOPOLITICS

RETHINKING
GEOPOLITICS

—m—

Jeremy Black

INDIANA UNIVERSITY PRESS

This book is a publication of

Indiana University Press
Office of Scholarly Publishing
Herman B Wells Library 350
1320 East 10th Street
Bloomington, Indiana 47405 USA

iupress.org

Manufactured in the United States of America

First printing 2024

Cataloging information is available from the Library of Congress.

ISBN 978-0-253-07161-3 (hardback)
ISBN 978-0-253-07163-7 (paperback)
ISBN 978-0-253-07162-0 (web PDF)

For
Billy Challis

CONTENTS

PREFACE

THE SPUR FOR THIS BOOK is the 120th anniversary, in 2024, of Halford Mackinder's seminal talk about geopolitics, the global "pivot," the Eurasian "heartland," and the change he discerned from the primacy of maritime to railborne land power; although, as a warning about further transformation, an audience member also mentioned the new age of air. This anniversary provides an opportunity to offer a short and accessible study, on geopolitics, its origins, history, and the present situation.

In contrast to my lengthy 2016 Indiana University Press book on geopolitics that included much on the situation prior to Mackinder, I want to start with him and to argue that he faced the same problem as modern US commentators: Britain was the great power in 1904, but its political, military, and economic primacy was under serious challenge and from more than one power, indeed from the United States, Russia, and Germany, all growing economies and expansionist states.

So also in 2024 for the United States and the challenges it confronts, notably from China but also from the very volatility of a global system in which US leadership is under great challenge, as, more generally, is the civilizational model of and from the West. Indeed, China deliberately sets out to contest US international models, seeing the United States' global liberalism as a challenge to national sovereignty, as well as being self-interested, with China presenting instead the Communist model of "managed socialism."

At the same time, the United States itself is very divided by the question of engagement with the outside world, as well as the nature of prioritization in strategic areas and tasks, for example, competing commitments to Taiwan, Ukraine, and the Middle East. This is a prioritization that sees geopolitics in action. In part, the use of geopolitics in this context is an aspect of the debate about prioritization, one that is rhetorical as well as analytical. This then sets the stage for a consideration of the 120 years from Mackinder to now, as well as geopolitics present and geopolitics future.

There are clear parallels between past British and present US geopolitical issues. Thus, in 1883, William Henry Smith, a Conservative politician, who had been First Lord of the Admiralty in 1877–80, spoke to the House of Commons about "the duties to be discharged by the Navy, and which are of a very varying nature throughout the world, because heavier duties fall upon the Navy of this country than fall upon the Navies of all other countries taken together. We have a large commerce, and practically we have to perform what are called the police duties of the seas, and we have, in consequence, to maintain an ironclad Fleet equal to any emergency."[1] This he explained later that year was difficult: "At this moment, ironclads have to be employed in the China and Australian Seas, in the Pacific, on the Coast of North America, and in the West Indies. Our Fleet is scattered in a manner in which the Fleet of no other power can be scattered; and while it is discharging duties in three or four different seas, if, unfortunately, we should be engaged in a war, Foreign Powers might be able to concentrate their forces against our Navy."[2] Comparable issues were to face Britain and the United States as leading powers.

In this and other contexts, whether "geopolitics" demands a formal input of geographical theory and knowledge or, indeed, what can be defined as geopolitics are matters for discussion. In part, geopolitics is another aspect of the role of human geography as aiding the understanding and use of physical geography. Geopolitics has been extended considerably in recent analysis, not least to include a trilogy of geopolitical constructs, subjects, and landscapes all operating in terms of the interaction of agents and structures in a fashion that is not deterministic but also not atomistic or diffuse.[3] Geopolitics is also a variant of the geography of strategy as it seeks more explicitly to engage, persuade, and instruct the public. A lack of agreement over definitions is shared with such other terms as *strategy* and *realpolitik*.[4] Allowing for this fundamental flaw, theory creates opportunities for commentators and notably so if it rests on vague definitions and propositions.

Geopolitics is polysemous, capable of having differing meanings, not least in rhetorical terms. Indeed, it overlaps greatly with what used to be called grand strategy, a term that is still employed, notably in the United States.[5] As with the earlier concept of the balance of power, geopolitics is useful precisely because it is imprecise, as context and content, being both descriptive and prescriptive and, as a linked point, describing what is allegedly natural and what has to be worked toward.

In addition, geoculture can play a role, with the work in particular of Samuel Huntington. Theory also seeks to provide an alternative to the ad hoc nature of developments. Indeed, geopolitical arguments provide a way to explain and justify specific policies and strategies in the short term and, as such, to try to ground the sense of advantage or threat in the short term in a rhetoric of longer-term necessity. Policy and rhetoric should not be starkly differentiated for there is a considerable overlap. Yet, at the same time, geopolitical arguments frequently fail to differentiate adequately between short-, medium-, and long-term requirements, needs, threats, and opportunities and between positive and negative goals and capabilities. The subject-object relation is frequently unclear: geopolitics is both subject (influences, actors) and object (affected by events and actors); and the latter alters geopolitical concepts. Thus, geopolitics in practice is a feedback loop that is at once self-definitional, reactive, and malleable. Far from being a major intellectual discipline, geopolitics is really an adjunct to political, diplomatic, and military studies.

Geopolitics indeed is a term sprayed like shrapnel across the geographical and historical landscapes and the landscape as a whole. It extends to fiction as in Tom Clancy's *Red Storm Rising* (1985), P. W. Singer and August Cole's *Ghost Fleet: A Novel of the Next World War* (2015), and Richard Shirreff's *War with Russia* (2016). It is also a term that has proved of growing popularity over the last decade, with no sign that this is likely to lessen. Works such as Robert Kaplan's *The Revenge of Geography: What* the Map Tells Us about Coming Conflicts and the Battle against Fate (2013) were published by major publishers, in this case Random House. Publishers certainly found the term useful.

The sense of a return to geopolitics was captured widely, including in book titles that really dealt with other subjects, for example, the English edition of Henrik Meinander's biography of Mannerheim: *Mannerheim, Marshal of Finland: A Life in Geopolitics* (2023). The publication of the English edition was reviewed in the *Times* with the remark that its timing "could hardly be better ... a point when geopolitics is in a state of upheaval."[6]

It is instructive to note that the literature surrounding geopolitics includes a utopian element. Thus, the proposed *Palgrave Handbook of Contemporary Geopolitics* (2024) moves from analysis to utopianism: "The Handbook highlights the wider strategic, economic, cultural and security geography of contemporary international relations. The Handbook of Contemporary Geopolitics bridges the gap between geopolitics, geoeconomics, global security, and strategy, to present analysis that points a way towards democratic, sustainable, and peaceful global development."[7]

Furthermore, it was and remains certainly the case that the extensive range of discussants was such that there was no control of terms by those expounding geopolitical theory. Thus, the lead essay in the *New York Review of Books* of August 12, 2015, was by the powerful financier George Soros and proposed a financial aspect to what he saw as "global disorder": "The future course of history will greatly depend on how China trades its economic transition from investment and export-led growth to greater dependence on domestic demand, and how the US reacts to it. A strategic partnership between us and China could prevent the evolution of two power blocks that may be drawn into military conflict."[8]

In this and other cases, whether the idea of rival geographical blocs constitute a geopolitical image or a metaphor that helps unlock geopolitical resonances for readers can be debated. It is certainly the case that there is no fixity or definition of the subject in terms of formal theory.

Indeed, in an instructive instance of definitional looseness, geopolitics is frequently employed with scant attention to geography however defined. For example, the Centre for Geopolitics at the University of Cambridge in its annual report of 2020 declared its mission in the following terms: "Providing historically-grounded solutions to enduring geopolitical problems." Throughout the report, there is no analysis of the characteristics of geopolitics nor indeed any sign that there is a geographical dimension to the center beyond places such as China, the Middle East, or "Britain's place in the world." Geography in short was/is location, not context, nor, indeed, dynamic in such accounts. The use of the term *geopolitics* by such bodies can be seen as facile.

This is not a criticism but simply an observation of the loose nature of both subject and vocabulary and indeed the frequent role of geopolitics as rhetorical stick-on rather than as a mode of analysis. Indeed, that rhetorical value and stick-on usage is what makes geopolitics so useful and therefore commonplace. Human agency in short is the key point. This means complexity in policy and problems in analysis. A key variable in geopolitical analysis is the amount of attention devoted to the danger, as understood by contemporaries or not, about division within the geopolitical space of particular states. It is easiest to build these divisions into the equation if they take the overt form of civil conflict, especially insurgency and counterinsurgency struggles calling on international support. Yet that is less typical than a more sustained sense that domestic policy is required to forestall dissidence and to build up strength, capability, and common purpose. In the case of the latter, progressivist policies were the norm, whatever the ideology: politics was a matter of competing analyses of improvability and programs for improvement. Thus, Halford Mackinder's Liberal Unionists fundamentally sought to strengthen the British Empire.

It is necessary to understand the interrelationship between countries' internal social policies and their perceptions of geopolitics. Thus, the need for Xi Jinping to strengthen Communist influence over Chinese society during the last eleven years has affected or is operating in tandem with his changing attitudes toward the outside world.

Separately, geopolitics is classically about space, not time, but changes affecting the latter, whether in terms of capabilities or of more specific operational success, influence the understanding of space and, in particular, its respective value in the geopolitical calculus. Thus, for example, the relative protection space provided the Russian "Heartland" in 1941–45 was lessened immediately after by the development of a US nuclear-armed aircraft capability. This remapped the territorial constraints of warfare and its time dimension, such that any conflict might close rapidly. Yet much geopolitical commentary did not engage adequately with this point.

The extent to which geoeconomic factors played a role in detailed strategic planning and more generally in geopolitics is difficult to assess. In part, there are the issues posed by the multiplicity of arguments and therefore documents that frequently (although not always) surround decisions. As a result, it is possible to advance interpretations that differ as well as simply overlap. At the same time, there is usually a coalition of interests behind a strategy, and it is not unreasonable to see differences as compatible. An instance is the British 1915 Dardanelles campaign, which can be seen in terms of navalism and the indirect approach, an alternative to the western front, and also as an attempt to open up a route for Russian wheat exports, thus helping address the rising cost of grain and Britain's need for Russia to address its financial issues.[9] The parallel with the current Ukraine crisis is instructive.

To a cynic, geopolitics as a thesis may be seen as a substitute for detailed archival work. More positively, it can be presented as a way to help shape the latter. That might be counterintuitive, and any idea that geography is somehow an independent, structural force is one that has to be used with great care. Indeed, the idea of an Anthropocene period in which human activity has been the dominant influence on the planet was extensively advanced beginning in the 2000s and has been applied to the decades from the 1950s on. Traces of plutonium released by nuclear weapons testing in the 1950s appear in relevant sites such as Crawford Lake in Canada.

Far from there being "enduring problems," it is differing contexts that are most notable, in the present as they were in the past. Geopolitics was related to population increases but in different ways. In the two world wars, there was an availability of very large forces and therefore an ability to cope with very large casualties, as the Soviet Union did in 1941 and Germany in 1944, and then fight on. These forces were far larger than those available for international conflict now, and that has an impact on the ability both to sustain attritional warfare between conventional forces and to conduct counterinsurgency conflict.

Geopolitics plays a major role in an account of international relations devoted to competition and strife. It assumes power relationships that have a spatial character, indeed drive, and can readily be seen as spatially driven. This, moreover, is the case whether conventional great-power geopolitics is concerned or the more radical and more sociological "critical geopolitics." As such, geopolitical thinking may itself encourage rivalry.

Ironically, although geopolitics is more commonly deployed with reference to international relations, notably as a form of a hidden hand explaining situations, developments, and warnings and particularly at the global level, this is not always helpful or pertinent. Thus, although many regions were put under pressure from external great powers, emergent local forces can also be a major problem. Indeed, it is mistaken to think of geopolitics without giving due weight to perspectives that are not those of the major powers.[10] For example, having lost its territorial access to the Pacific in the War of the Pacific in 1879–82, Bolivia's foreign policy was dominated by a search for renewed access of some form.[11]

Geopolitics, furthermore, is highly pertinent and frequent at the domestic/internal level. Thus, analyses of US politics in terms of red or blue states or urban areas to explain voting trends or, indeed, law and order or other variables have a clear geographical component. So also with the political elements of transport links, for example, differential support for Amtrak in the United States or the drive by states to create new capitals and administrative centers, as currently in Egypt. The degree to which such an assessment of domestic geopolitics contributes to the broader discussion of geopolitics at the international level is at best indirect. This is a major flaw. In practice, there are major links. Thus, the degree of alleged Russian meddling in the 2016 presidential campaign affected some US geopolitical perceptions about Russia. Moreover, in this and other instances, the situation is being made dynamic by the internet and social media, the latter contributing to the complex relationships between geopolitics, perception, and misperception. These will be taken further by the development of AI (artificial intelligence).

Thus, geopolitics, the geographical dimensions of power and politics, is present at a number of scales and does not have a fixed meaning. That is the reason behind its usage in this book as a signifier of geographical links rather than as a precise analytical device. That this is also the general usage, whatever the formal requirements of theory, is highly pertinent.

I have benefited greatly from the comments on an earlier draft by John Brobst, Pete Brown, Alice Catherine Carls, Bill Gibson, Ken Weisbrode, and Anthony Wells; from discussions with Tony King, Oliver Letwin, Steve Smith, and Richard Wylde; and from the opportunity to speak at the Foreign Policy Research Institute in Philadelphia, to give the opening plenary lecture at the 2022 annual conference of the Baltic Defence College, and to speak for the Eisenhower Library in 2023; for the Calpe conference in Gibraltar in 2023, for the 2022 and 2023 Warfare and Strategy courses of the Republic of Indonesia Defence University, and to give a series of sixteen podcasts held on the website of the *Critic* magazine. It is a great pleasure to dedicate this book to Billy Challis, a wise observer of the present-day world whose friendship is much appreciated.

RETHINKING
GEOPOLITICS

ONE

LIBERAL UNIONIST GEOPOLITICS AND MACKINDER

GEOPOLITICS AS GEOGRAPHICAL DESTINY WAS a theme of much literature, notably but not only popular works in the early twenty-first century and, more particularly, during both the "war on terror" and in response to rising great power animosity involving the United States, China, and Russia. While apparently plausible, this viewpoint, however, is misguided, for it downplays the role of human agency. Indeed, humans not only perceive and interpret their geographical context but can also change it. Transoceanic expansion exemplified this point, as in the long-range voyages that established human settlement in the Pacific. Subsequently, the European "voyages of exploration" created new geographical routes, for example, round southern Africa to South Asia and from Mexico to the Philippines. Engineering also served to create new marine routes, notably with the Suez (1869) and Panama (1914) Canals.

With the politics of nodes and routes, there is a tendency to see places and links in static terms, as in the British naval base in Malta and the Suez Canal, but there could be both improvements and changes in vulnerability and protection. Thus, in the 1880s, there was interest in torpedo-carrying warships, and this put pressure on the idea of a close blockade. Indeed, it ensured an interest in defensible advanced bases to reduce fleet vulnerability to torpedo attack. At the same time, the geopolitics of power projection was affected beginning in the late nineteenth century by the use of breech loaders, rifled artillery, percussion detonators, and high explosives, all of which affected the possibilities for naval bombardment. This serves as a reminder that the lines on the map, in this case the coastline, have varied meanings in terms of their defensibility, a point that subsequently greatly expanded with the use of air attack and missiles.

The human creation of new routes has been advancing this century at breakneck speed, with transformative change both designed, as with the Chinese rail program, and in part independent of direct human intention, as with global warming opening up Arctic sea routes. In turn, emphasizing political choice, the military, political, and economic possibilities of the opening up of Arctic sea routes are being probed by Russia and discussed by other powers, including China.

There is also the extent to which the very perception of geopolitical realities, whether or not seen as unchanging, is shot through with political assumptions and commitments whatever the pretense of objectivity. Moreover, this process extends to those who comment on geopolitics, including obviously myself. No writer is free in some form of Olympian detachment or can offer oracular judgment. Instead, it is important to note the degree to which analysis is part of the wider politics of geopolitics, indeed a key constituent of the latter.

And also with the British academic Halford Mackinder (1861–1947). He was not the first to coin the term *geopolitics*. That, in 1899, was a Swede, Rudolf Kjellén (1864–1922). Kjellén, very much a political figure, was influenced by a German, Friedrich Ratzel (1844–1904). The latter had stressed the close relationship of people and environment in a competitive international system in a number of books, notably *Politische Geographie* (1897), and was to be influential on the German Right, not least with the concept of *Lebensraum*, or living space.

The key German geopolitical applier of the next generation, Karl Haushofer (1869–1946), was influenced by Ratzel, whom he had met. As an example of the intellectual ferment of the developing subject, Haushofer was also influenced by the ideas of Kjellén, Mackinder, and Mahan, as well as by his stay in Japan. Indeed, Haushofer saw Japanese expansionism as an example for Germany. He was, in practice, a social Darwinian, convinced by organic theories of the rise and fall of states. These organic theories were racist in their content because the state was presented as a racial construction and expression, one that was given organic identity not by constitutional development but by the health and character of a given people. There was therefore a vitalist character to the analysis and rivalry, one that played out across a geographical background, in the sense of territorially located peoples, but that otherwise did not have a geographical explanation.

At the same time, that perspective did not foreordain more specific ideas of the application of such a conviction. For Haushofer, as for others, organic notions, such as *Lebensraum*, coexisted with more practical, mechanistic ideas of how to pursue political, military, and commercial advantage, for example, by maritime policies. The last was seen with naval races[1] and with such publications as Haushofer's book *World Seas and World Powers* (1937).[2]

Like Haushofer, Mackinder was a political player, but they were different in both context and content. He was particularly significant as the leading geopolitical commentator of the world's most powerful empire and foremost naval power, with the expression of ideas that can be called political aspects of the debates over both empire and navy. A well-connected academic, who became director of the London School of Economics from 1903 to 1908, Mackinder was an unsuccessful parliamentary candidate in 1900 and 1909 but an MP (member of Parliament) from 1910 until 1922. His subsequent posts included high commissioner to South Russia in 1919–20, at a time of British intervention; chairman of the Imperial Shipping Committee in 1920–45; and chairman of the Imperial Economic Committee in 1925–31.

The failed intervention in the Russian Civil War, an intervention Mackinder supported, may be regarded as more widely indicative and has been presented as such by those aware of the long-term hostility with the Soviet Union / Russia that has lasted to the present. However, the Whites whom Britain supported were divided, the Bolsheviks (Communists) had important structural advantages in the conflict, and the Western states and publics were exhausted by World War I.[3] Certainly then, Mackinder was somewhat short on practicality.

Mackinder had moved to join the Conservatives in 1903 but, prior to that, was one of their allied Liberal Unionists. His politics can be seen in terms of the latter and their major contribution to the Conservatives. Indeed, more generally, Liberal Unionism was an aspect of the development of British geopolitics, and elements of it looked to its US successor.

The contemporary influence of Mackinder's views is a matter for discussion, with one member of his audience on January 25, 1904, regretting the absence of those powerful in government. In part, the nature of the British imperial state increased the possibilities for the impact of external ideas. There was a relative lack of administrative and intellectual institutions for imperial planning and defense. At the same time, there was growing interest in both, and the circles of intellectual opinion sustained through meetings in London, including in clubland, provided many opportunities for building up and on this interest. Mackinder's metropolitan milieu was very much part of this process. Pressure was linked to speculation by the established sense of the power Britain should wield and the anxiety about its ability to do so in a changing world.

That, however, does not mean that there were not alternative strands to British geopolitics nor that Liberal Unionism itself was homogenous. In essence it arose from a Liberal split, specifically over the terms of keeping Ireland within the British Empire, with a tranche of Liberal opinion breaking from the Liberal Party under its leader W. E. Gladstone in opposing the latter's determination to introduce "home rule" or effective autonomy. The Liberal Unionists joined the Conservatives in opposing this measure and thus used imperial identity as the key issue on which to resist the increasingly radical, indeed left-wing, nature of the Liberal Party. The latter divided further for a while over the response to British involvement in war with the Boer (Afrikaner) republics of South Africa in

1899–1902, with the Liberal Unionists again solidly in support of the Conservatives. This war was one in which many key figures were involved in support of the imperial commitment, from Winston Churchill to Arthur Conan Doyle, and as part of a commitment to a Greater Britain that drew in part on ideas of partnership based on settler Dominions and a British race and identity.[4] The Liberal Party was to split anew over the politics of World War I.

It was not only in Britain that geopolitics had a pronounced political slant. So also in other countries, and not least due to the careers, expenditure, and economic interests bound up in the particular choices made, for example, by the East Coast manufacturing interests, notably Pennsylvania shipyards and steelworks, involved in the US naval buildup.[5] This growth both contributed to a navalist slant in US geopolitics and was a product of it. This navalism was given a historicized geopoliticism in the works of Alfred Thayer Mahan and was particularly significant when Theodore "Teddy" Roosevelt was president (1901–9).

In France, a major imperial power, the naval establishment was mostly monarchist, a position unacceptable to the governments of the Third Republic. They supported the ideas of the Jeune École and Admiral Théophile Aube, author of *La Guerre Maritimes et Les Ports Françaises* (1882), who favored not battleships but faster unarmored light cruisers able to attack the commerce of opponents.[6] Whatever the technology or politics, the rhetoric of "command of the sea" remained significant, as goal and/or target.

Mackinder's reiterated calls for a Greater Britain were in practice part of a debate in which ideas of imperial defense, his commitment, clashed with the determination of the Dominions to cooperate from a position of considerable autonomy. Military independence was part of the equation for Dominion leaders, and notably so in Australia.[7] Mackinder's centripetal emphasis on a commonality of geopolitical pressure made sense of a British alliance with Japan and with the long-term buildup of a "Greater India" to resist Russia but scarcely accorded with variations that included Australasian and Canadian concerns about Japan and the United States respectively, South African interest in expansion in southern Africa, and Indian engagement with strategic concerns from East Africa to China, as well as relations with Russia.

In their writings, their politics, and their lives, both Churchill and Doyle showed a commitment to imperial geopolitics. Indeed, their works indicate the cultural grounding and expression of geopolitical themes. Those of Churchill are well known, but Doyle stood twice for Parliament, in 1900 and 1906; he and Mackinder both stood unsuccessfully in 1906, a year of Liberal triumph. Both wanted to see a strengthening at home and imperial development. As an example of other parallels, each was also interested in medicine and the relationship of diseases to environmental conditions.

Popular writing is very instructive, because there is a tendency to see geopolitics solely in intellectual terms and, more particularly, with reference to works in which the subject and method are formally introduced. This is mistaken. Instead, the situation, at least in part, can be reversed. Geopolitical ideas are most effective and therefore significant when they enter popular culture and become part of the resulting habit of thought. This habit can lead to a reflexive tendency to advance particular tropes when geographical ideas are expressed. The most obvious are

the sense that propinquity or distance create a basic duality around which issues of threat and interest are created
or structured. Secondly comes the application of particular characteristics to specific peoples, these characteristics
being associated with the specific areas that gave them
identity and, supposedly, personality and goals. This was a
long-standing geopolitical conception, one that goes back
in the Western tradition to Greek views of other peoples.
As also with China, there was a structuring of space, with
those outside being "barbarians" who were thereby deciv-
ilized and requiring blandishments or control.

This approach has survived to the present, notably in
ideas underlying the supposed "war of civilizations" between religious groups and with domestic equivalents
including "culture wars." At the same time, there is a different geopolitics, one that is not value absent but that
treats states and people as of equal merit in a "realist" interpretation of international relations.

Empire is always present in the world of Sherlock
Holmes as created by Doyle, which, thereby, was very dif-
ferent from the US geopolitical assumptions discussed
in chapters 4 and 5. For Doyle, London is the center of
imperial networks, and empire is a source of renewal and
material wealth for Britain, one that gives the latter depth.
This is very much seen in *The Hound of the Baskervilles*. Sir
Charles's wealth comes from the South African goldfields.
Before his successor, Sir Henry Baskerville, returns to
Britain, the young baronet has spent his entire adult life in
Canada on the prairies, and he represents youth, virility,
and a confidence in the future also seen in the Australian-
born characters in the stories, and a vigor indicated by the
lack of smartly dressing "the part" that Sir Henry, when

returning to Britain, has to remedy by purchasing new clothes and boots. Alongside the occasional flaw, the idea of imperial masculinity as noble was frequently presented in Holmes stories, as with the Australian sea captain in "The Abbey Grange" (1904): "Our door was opened to admit as fine a specimen of manhood as ever passed through it. He was a very tall young man, golden-moustached, blue-eyed, with a skin which had been burned by tropical suns, and a springy step which showed that the huge frame was as active as it was strong."

Captain Croker in that story uses the commonplace language of empire, addressing Holmes's requirement that he come clean about events: "I believe you are a man of your word, and a white man," the latter a racist commonplace for being honest. Manliness, more generally, was a matter not only of supporting the cause of imperial federalism but also of serving in the army or, at least, volunteering.

In contrast, Doyle's treatment of the Andaman Islanders as savage reflects the sense of civilizational conflict and progress and also the defense of British imperialism. This approach was seen also in his non-Holmes work *The Tragedy of the Korosko*, which appeared as a serial in *The Strand Magazine* in 1897, as a book in 1898, and, in an adaptation by Doyle, as the play *Fires of Fate* (1909), which, in 1923, became a film. The story is very much set in the here and now of the British conflict with the Mahdists of Sudan and thus had a geopolitical immediacy even more striking than Mackinder's 1904 lecture. In the novel, Cecil Brown presents the "Dervishes" (Mahdists) as uncompromising believers in destiny, the proof of how bigotry leads toward barbarism, and a dire threat to the civilization of Egypt, which since the invasion of 1882 is protected by Britain.

The latter is an instance of the thesis of the "translation of empires" with imperial states succeeding to the mission and position of others. This was particularly attractive to Britain, which saw itself as the modern Rome, while Russia looked to Byzantium, and Germany and Japan to earlier periods of imperial power. Civilizational models were crucial to this idea of geopolitics, as the claim to sway rested on a sense of destiny, albeit one that could be corrupted by indulgence, division, and social weakness. Later in the twentieth century, this idea was to be subsumed into a US geopolitics that drew on the idea of having to replace Britain in imperial status and commitments. This idea was significant to the US definition of geopolitical interests during the Cold War.

Brown feels that Britain has taken on the excessive burdens of being the global policeman, only for Colonel Cochrane to argue that he has

> a very limited view of our national duties . . . behind national interests and diplomacy and all that there lies a great guiding force—a Providence in fact—which is for ever getting the best out of each nation and using it for the good of the whole. When a nation ceases to respond, it is time that she went into hospital for a few centuries, like Spain or Greece—the virtue has gone out of her. A man or a nation is not placed upon the earth to do merely what is pleasant and what is profitable. . . . That is how we rule India. We came there by a kind of natural law, like air rushing into a vacuum.

There is also an opportunity for Doyle to advance his view of Anglo-American Manifest Destiny: "The English-speakers are all in the same boat. . . . We and you have among our best men a higher conception of moral sense and public duty than is to be found in any other people.... These are the two qualities which are needed for directing a weaker race. ... The pressure of destiny will force you to administer the Whole of America from Mexico to the Horn." The last was a geopolitical view of destiny that was held by many Americans.

A hero of empire featured in "The Devil's Foot," an effective Holmes story that was published in 1910 but set in 1897. The tall, craggy, fierce-eyed Leon Sterndale, "the great lion-hunter and explorer" with a "tremendous personality," kills the villainous Mortimer Tregennis with a rare West African ordeal poison he "obtained under very extraordinary circumstances in the Ubanghi country." Having in effect been his judge, Holmes, impressed by the "lawless lion-hunter," lets him go to central Africa to complete his work. This was national character as geopolitical destiny.

Explorers, indeed, were famous in Britain and the West, literally, it was believed, creating geographical knowledge as they advanced civilization and displayed national character. Henry Morton Stanley (1841–1904), who had made his fame as an explorer of central Africa, was the Liberal Unionist MP for Lambeth North in 1895–1900, having been defeated for the seat by a Liberal by a narrow margin in 1892. Ernest Shackleton, the polar explorer and an Anglo-Irishman opposed to Irish home rule, was an unsuccessful Liberal Unionist candidate for Dundee in 1906.

The heyday of the Holmes stories marked a high point in London's grand imperial history. London provided the setting for Victoria's Golden and Diamond Jubilees in 1887 and 1897. Prominent visitors, such as the Khedive of Egypt in 1900, were entertained by the mayor and

corporation of the city. Whitehall had grand new minis-
terial buildings, notably the New War Office (1899–1906)
and the New Public Offices (1899–1915). The Mall was
conceived as a great ceremonial route with, at one end,
Buckingham Palace's new facade as well as the enormous
Victoria memorial in the *rond-point* in front of the palace
and, at the other, Admiralty Arch (1912), which provided
an opening onto Trafalgar Square and the north end of
Whitehall. This was a geopolitics of urban planning for
the display of power.

Doyle was far from alone in his subjects and attitudes.
Sudan was to the fore for many writers. A. E. W. Mason's
The Four Feathers, a successful novel of 1902, was a presentation of British operations in Sudan as a definition of
manliness and heroism. Mason was elected to Parliament
in 1906 as a Liberal, sitting until 1910, and served in the
army and in naval intelligence in World War I.

Sudan also appeared in the adventure stories for boys
by the war correspondent George Alfred Henty. These
included *The Dash for Khartoum: A Tale of the Nile Expedition* (1891); two on the Boer War, *With Buller in Natal*
(1900) and *With Roberts to Pretoria* (1901); and *With Kitchener in the Soudan* (1902), which in effect brought to completion the 1891 account. Henty presented the conquest
of Sudan as a "stupendous achievement," declaring in the
preface, "Thus a land that had been turned into a desert by
the terrible tyranny of the Mahdi and his successor, was
wrested from barbarism and restored to civilization; and
the stain upon British honour, caused by the desertion of
Gordon by the British ministry of the day, was wiped out,"
the last a reference to the events of 1885 when Khartoum

had fallen to the Mahdists and its commander, Charles Gordon, killed.

British expansion was thereby presented as valuable in a civilizational sense. The emphasis was not on thwarting French expansion, which, in the Fashoda Crisis of 1898, nearly led to conflict between the two powers. In this case, axes of interest and expansion were seen as in competition, a fundamental geopolitical device. Thus, Britain was interested in north-south expansion from Egypt via Sudan to central Africa, meeting in Uganda a new axis of expansion inland from Kenya and, maybe, linking up with a northward axis from South Africa. In contrast, there was a west-east axis of French interest in the Sahel, just as farther south there was a Portuguese one to join the colonies of Angola and Mozambique.

As with so many stories of the period, including the Holmes stories and Mason's *Four Feathers*, there was a mystery as part of the narrative of *With Kitchener in the Soudan*, in this case the protagonist's background. The story finally reveals that he is entitled to the title and estates of the Marquess of Langdale. Exemplary manliness was part of the geopolitics.

A different form of heroism was offered by Churchill in *The River War: An Historical Account of the Reconquest of the Soudan* (1899). This provided a clear account of the British defeat of the Mahdists: "They lived by the sword. Why should they not perish by the magazine rifle? A state of society which, even if it were tolerable to those whom it comprised, was an annoyance to civilised nations has been swept aside. . . . The Government was a cruel despotism."[8]

While some acquisitions such as Uganda were made with reluctance on the part of many ministers, much British imperial expansion, especially in 1880–1914, arose directly from the response to the real or apparent plans of other powers, particularly France and Russia, both of whom were expanding rapidly and also becoming allies. This was an aspect of the ad hoc and impoverished character of imperialism also seen with other powers, one in which local conditions and specific moments played a role.[9] However, the search for markets for British industry was also important. Thus, both economic and political security were at stake; and, as a result, the imperialist surge of activity at the close of the century has been seen as marking the beginning of a long decline from the zenith of British power, and of imperial position starting to fray under pressure at the same time that it continued to expand and, thereby, encounter additional problems. This underlines the complexities of geopolitical context.

The nature of the British Empire, and of others, also changed. Sovereignty and territorial control became crucial goals, replacing the pursuit of influence and of island and port possessions, which had been the characteristic features of much, although by no means all, British expansion earlier in the nineteenth century. Suspicion of Russian designs on the Turkish Empire and of French schemes in North Africa led the British to move into Cyprus (1878) and Egypt (1882); concern about French ambitions in Southeast Asia resulted in the conquest of Mandalay (1885) and the annexation of Upper Burma (1886); while Russia's advance across Central Asia led to attempts to strengthen and move forward the "North-West Frontier" of British India and also to the development of

British influence in southern Iran and the Persian Gulf, through which the British routed the telegraph to India. French and German expansion in Africa led Britain to take countermeasures, in Gambia, Sierra Leone, the Gold Coast (Ghana), Nigeria, and Uganda, all moves in the "scramble for Africa" by the European powers. Doyle was far more interested in southern Africa and Sudan and clearly saw them as more noble tasks than expansion in West Africa. Britain's opponents in both were certainly stronger and had earlier been successful, the Boers in 1881 in the First Boer War and the Mahdists in 1885. Each remained formidable opponents and was not overcome until 1900–1902 and 1898–99 respectively.

Specific clashes over colonial influence with other European powers increasingly interacted, beginning in the late 1870s, with a more general sense of imperial insecurity, as British confidence was put under pressure by the growing strength of other states. More clearly, in the 1880s, there was public and governmental concern about naval vulnerability, and, in 1889, this concern led to the Naval Defence Act, which sought a two-power standard: superiority over the next two largest naval powers combined. The importance of naval dominance was taken for granted. It was a prerequisite of an ideal of national self-sufficiency that peaked in the late nineteenth century. The geopolitics of naval concern and commitment was very dependent on the strength of the navy. Thus, again, geography was part of a system and not an independent determinant. Indeed, the challenges of naval commitment were dependent not so much on geography as on the strength, moves, and apparent intentions of other powers. Yet geography was also significant in terms of the naval protection of trade and empire, notably by means of "relays" of power, especially naval bases and coaling depots. In consequence, the movement and speed of individual warships could be converted into planned action at the will of the center. As advocated in 1881–82 in reports produced by the Carnarvon Commission,[10] the extension of the network of British coaling stations ensured that their steam-powered armored warships could be used in waters across the world. The British also controlled many of the world's colliers. The circumnavigation of the world by the "Great White Fleet" in 1907–9 revealed that the US fleet could not cross the Pacific without British coal. Other powers also established naval bases, such as those of France, including Martinique, Guadeloupe, Dakar, Libreville, Gabon, Diego Suarez, Obok, Saigon, and Kwangchouwan. Russia developed ports at Darien and Port Arthur to strengthen its position in Manchuria.

Geopolitics as advanced by Mackinder made much of the distinction between continental and oceanic states, an emphasis also seen with Mahan. In part, this approach rested on a British self-image, but Mackinder was aware that in practice the Greater Britain imperium included continental power, and notably so with India and its massive army. Moreover, while Australia was an island, it was also in effect a subcontinent, and, by 1904, it was difficult to think of Canada or the British possessions in South Africa as different in this respect to Australia.

This point has a longer resonance. Thus, the understandings of sea power advanced more recently reflected in part the flexibility of geopolitical arguments or, looked at differently, their weakness. For example, the states with the two leading navies in the 2020s, the United States and

China, would strike most commentators as sea powers but were not in the definition advanced in 2018 by Andrew Lambert, who instead emphasized maritime identity, the embrace of change, and geopolitical aspiration. Lambert separated sea from land states, which led to some curious exclusions, as well as the simplification into one strategic culture and geopolitical aspiration of countries that had a range including both continental and maritime elements. These countries included early modern Portugal, late seventeenth-century France, Japan from the Meiji Restoration to 1945, and the United States.[11]

Geopolitics was also seen in titles and naming. Empire Day was launched in 1896 on May 24, Victoria's birthday. While, in 1871, having defeated France, Wilhelm I, king of Prussia, became emperor of Germany, Victoria, five years later, as a result of the Royal Titles Act, became empress of India—an empire that was to last until the subcontinent was granted independence in 1947, with the title being inherited by her four successors. To harness popular opinion and as an aspect of human geopolitics, streets, towns, geographical features, and whole tracts of land were named or renamed in her honor, including the Australian state of Victoria, the city of Victoria on Vancouver Island in Canada, Victoria Falls on the Zambezi, and Lake Victoria in East Africa. So also with the naming of places after other members of the royal family and after British politicians, for example, Salisbury in Southern Rhodesia, now Harare in Zimbabwe.

In the long-established colonies of white settlement, as aspects of the Greater Britain, self-government was extended beginning in the mid-nineteenth century, with the growth of what was called "responsible government."

This constitutional aspect of British imperial geopolitics meant that, in a major measure of liberalization, colonial governors were to be politically responsible to locally elected legislatures rather than to London, a process that reflected the comparable parliamentary arrangement in Victorian Britain. The counterpart of responsible government was the psychological and physical self-reliance Doyle gives his colonials visiting Britain and meeting Holmes.

In the contemporary case of the US "empire," a description made more commonly by foreigners than by Americans, there was a differently constituted system of responsible government, with (some) territories translated into states. This consolidated the coast-to-coast expansion of the nineteenth century but was not extended more widely, in part for racist reasons, as with Puerto Rico, conquered from Spain in 1898. Variety was to be a continuing theme, with Alaska and Hawaii becoming states and many Pacific islands, notably the Philippines, independent, while other possessions continued to be territories.

For the British Empire, Dominion status, self-government under the Crown, offered a peaceful, evolutionary route to independence. Canada became a Dominion in 1867, Australia in 1901, and New Zealand in 1907. Although the Colonial Laws Validity Act of 1865 had declared invalid any colonial legislation that clashed with that from Westminster, the act was only rarely invoked. This was a federalism that worked, and those were models for the possible transfer of empires into federative polities, with a different geopolitical identity and a greater strength. Meetings of prime ministers beginning in 1887 helped give the Dominions a voice in imperial policy and also offered a means of coherence. During the Boer War (1899–1902), the empire, particularly Australia, Canada, Cape Colony, and New Zealand, sent troops to help the British forces, actions that fostered Dominion nationalism within the empire rather than having this nationalism act as a separatist element.

Yet, alongside expansion and changes designed both to mold and to benefit from the situation of flux in the empire, cracks were appearing in the imperial edifice. Due in part to the diffusion within it of British notions of community, identity, and political action, there was a measure of opposition to imperial control, with the Indian National Congress formed in 1885 and the Egyptian National Party in 1897. As a result, the geopolitical reality of the empire was open to debate.

The most immediate challenge to empire, the Boer War, was waged with the Afrikaner (Boer, i.e., whites of Dutch descent) republics of the Orange Free State and the Transvaal in southern Africa. Regional hegemony was a key issue. British leaders found it difficult to accept Boer views and were willing to risk war to achieve a transfer of some power in southern Africa. The Boer War is often seen as a classic instance of "capitalist-driven" empire building. However, Alfred Milner, the aggressive governor of Cape Colony, was essentially driven by political considerations, his own ambition, and his strong sense of imperial mission on behalf of a British race.[12] The British ministers were greatly influenced by the fear that if, given the gold and diamond discoveries, the Boers became the most powerful force in southern Africa, it might not be long before they were working with Britain's imperial rivals, especially the Germans in South-West Africa, and threatening her strategic interests at the Cape. The prime minister, Robert, 3rd Marquess of Salisbury, remarked that Britain had to be supreme. Ministers in London thought (wrongly) the Boers were bluffing and would not put up much of a fight if war followed; while the failure of the British to send sufficient reinforcements persuaded the Boers to think it was the British who were bluffing. The Boer republics declared war after Britain had isolated them internationally and had done everything possible to provoke them.[13] How this matches conventional geopolitical accounts is open to discussion.

Yet the background was of an apparently continuously expanding empire, a process that provided a particular psychological character to the geopolitical discussion of empire. In 1901, Asante was annexed, while an expeditionary force was sent to the interior of British Somaliland, to confront the rising by Sayyid Muhammad 'Abdille Hassan, who, in 1899, had declared holy war on Christians. By 1905, the British had forced a peace on their opponents. In 1903, the army of the Emirates of the Sokoto Caliphate was smashed at Burmi in northern Nigeria. The following year, a force advanced from India to Lhasa, the capital of Tibet, to thwart alleged Russian influence and dictate terms. In Kenya in 1905, tribal opposition was overcome. And so on. There was a strong degree of force underlying imperial expansion and consolidation.

And so also for other imperial powers both Western and non-Western, the latter including Turkey in Yemen and Abyssinia. Geopolitical ideas were advanced, although their significance may be problematic. In the case of Italy, the invasion of Libya in 1911 was defended on the grounds that it would secure the "Fourth Shore," the land across the Mediterranean, the other shores being those washed by the Tyrrhenian, Ionian, and Adriatic Seas.[14] Looked at differently, this was a justification for motives from grandeur and opportunity to seeking a place to settle Italians who would otherwise emigrate.

Opposition to British control or influence in the colonies and in the informal empire was still limited in scope, certainly in comparison to the situation after World War I; and there was also a considerable measure of compliance with British rule. In Ireland, the preferred option was home rule under the Crown, not republican independence, which, at the time, was the choice of only a minority. Meanwhile, Scots benefited greatly from the empire, while the degree to which they retained considerable independence within the United Kingdom—including their own established church and legal and educational systems—also militated against political nationalism.

The politics of the following years saw the same issues and alignments again come to the fore, and that situation was an aspect of the background to the deployment of British geopolitical thought. Indeed, in some respects, it was a stage and means in the shaping of debate about imperial content.

In 1904, Mackinder, the leading British geopolitician, argued in a lecture to the Royal Geographical Society in London that the railway had moved the balance from sea power to land power. He particularly justified the argument in terms of the Russian construction of the Trans-Siberian Railway on the pattern of transcontinental lines in North America but, he claimed, of greater geostrategic significance. Already, in his book *Britain and the British Seas* (1902), Mackinder had forcefully proposed that the development of rail technology and systems had altered the paradigm of economic potential away from maritime power. This view seemed borne out by US and German economic growth, both of which benefited greatly from the impact of rail, although each was also a major naval power. This had enabled the United States to crush Spain in 1898. Indeed, by 1909, US battleships were being designed with larger coal bunkers, allowing a steaming radius of ten thousand nautical miles.

In 1904, Mackinder claimed that the Trans-Siberian Railway made possible the movement of forces rapidly around a Eurasian "heartland" and "pivot," such that Russia could threaten its opponents, whether Japan in the Far East, British interests in India, or European rivals. Mackinder presented the "heartland" of Eurasia as "the pivot region of the world's politics, past, present, and future, and claimed that control over it would threaten other powers":

> Europe and European history . . . subordinate to Asia and Asiatic history, for European civilisation is . . . the outcome of the secular struggle against Asiatic invasions. . . . Russia replaces the Mongol Empire. Her pressure on Finland, on Scandinavia, on Poland, on Turkey, on Persia, on India, and on China, replaces the centrifugal raids of the steppeman. . . . I have spoken as a geographer. The actual balance of political power at any given time is, of course, the product, on the one hand, of the geographical conditions, both economic and strategic, and, on the other hand, of the relative number, virility, equipment, and organisation of the competing peoples.[15]

The latter implied reform by Britain and in the context of vigilance about possible international and domestic developments. Concern about Russian expansion was also expressed by the US commentator Alfred Thayer Mahan in his *The Problems of Asia: Its Effect upon International Politics* (1900), although it displayed the classic problem of pontification.[16]

Mackinder's ideas about rail and the "pivot" were unrealistic, because he exaggerated the capacity of rail; but he, like so many, was convinced that change had become possible. In his 1904 lecture, he argued that "a generation ago steam and the Suez Canal appeared to have increased the mobility of sea-power relative to land power," but "transcontinental railways are now transmuting the conditions of land-power."[17] He did not anticipate the degree to which ships remained more efficient means to transport bulk cargo—and that even before the containerization revolution that began in the 1950s further shifted the balance in favor of the economics of the sea—although Mackinder also argued that alliance between the naval powers could restrain those of continental Eurasia, an approach that linked an imperial Greater Britain, the United States, and Japan.[18]

At the time (and subsequently) commentators interested in rail and indeed geopolitics were apt to underplay the frictions of distance and issues of scale in terms of usage. As Robert, 3rd Marquess of Salisbury—then secretary of state for India, later prime minister—had pointed out in Parliament in 1877, the habit of looking at maps that misleadingly suggested proximity was a serious problem:

> I cannot help thinking that in discussions of this kind, a great deal of misapprehension arises from the popular use of maps on a small scale. As with such maps you are able to put a thumb on India and a finger on Russia, some persons

> at once think that the political situation is alarming and
> that India must be looked to. If the noble Lord would use a
> larger map—say one on the scale of the Ordnance Map of
> England—he would find that the distance between Russia
> and British India is not to be measured by the finger and
> thumb, but by a rule [i.e., ruler].[19]

No such map was available, but similar caveats could be
offered about many rail plans, and this remains the case.

Territorial expansion and interests, nevertheless, were
generally helped by rail. It served the interests both of
maritime states, such as Britain and France, looking to
develop colonies and overseas influence from port positions, and those of continental states, such as Russia,
seeking to exploit possibilities. Thus, beginning in 1879,
Russia constructed the Trans-Caspian Railway from
Uzun-Ada (later Krasnovodsk) on the eastern shore of
the Caspian Sea, to Merv in 1886, Samarkand in 1888, and
Tashkent in 1898, with a permanent bridge over the Oxus
(Amu Dar'ya) in 1901. This line was seen as consolidating
Russia's recently established position in Central Asia and
greatly worried the British in India. In 1900–1906, this
line was linked to the Russian system by the Tashkent or
Trans-Aral Railway, from Kinel to Tashkent. This could
move troops to Central Asia and cotton from there to
mills in Moscow.

Further east, in 1896, by the Li-Lobanov Treaty, the Russians obliged China to grant a concession for a Russian-
gauge railway to the Russian port of Vladivostok across
Manchuria (part of China), which was a more direct route
than one restricted to Russian territory. Russia had the
right to station troops to protect the railway, an important application of the idea that railways established an

interest that then had to be protected. As an aspect of the self-supporting or cumulative nature of geopolitics, this protection, in turn, was dependent on the railway and its ability to move troops. As a reminder of the need to differentiate between geopolitical interest, this argument for protection was more easily employed by states and on behalf of them rather than private companies, but governments could intervene on behalf of companies, as the US one was apt to do. The latter looks toward the question of the revival of a company-based geopolitics in recent years, with the close interests of national governments with oil companies, some of them state owned, such as the French company Elf-Aquitaine, now succeeded by big tech companies able to pursue policies as if independent.

For Russia, the territorial annexation of the Amur River territories in 1858–60 and the foundation of Vladivostok in 1860 was followed, after sweeping Japanese victory in the Sino-Japanese War of 1894–95, by expansion into Manchuria. This appeared to Russia a vacuum, into which, however, Russian overprojected itself. In accordance with the 1896 treaty, the Chinese Eastern Railway was constructed in 1897–1904, while in 1898 China granted a southern extension from Harbin to the port of Dalian (Port Arthur). When the Russians advanced against the Chinese in Manchuria in 1900, part of the crisis affecting China at the time of the Boxer Rebellion, the railway served as an axis of movement. This Chinese Eastern Railway proved a key means and issue of Russian power until it was purchased by Japan in 1934 and used instead by the Japanese. What was also called the Southern Manchurian Railway Company, whose concession Japan gained from Russia as a result of the Russo-Japanese War of 1904–5, had an attached right to administer the land alongside the railway. As a result, the company's work far exceeded the normal management of a railway.

The scope of the Russian rail system had become an issue during the war with Japan in 1904–5, in this case with the need to reinforce and sustain, across the vast distance of Siberia, the peripheral but strategically significant position in the Russian Far East and Manchuria against Japanese attack. As an instructive instance of the comparative nature of geopolitics, it had proved easier for Britain to use maritime links to reinforce its forces in South Africa during the Boer War than it was for Russia by land. Yet, although in 1904 the Trans-Siberian Railway, itself only a single track, was incomplete at Lake Baikal (across which ferries were used for a four-hour crossing, until the Circum-Baikal railway was completed in 1905), the Russians transported 370,000 troops along it to the east. Lake Baikal, the world's seventh-largest lake by surface area, has a maximum length of 395 miles and maximum width of 49 miles. However, the Russian ability to use the railways as an integrated element of strategy making has been queried: capacity did not feed through into a predicted movement of troops that was ably used for deployment-based operational planning.

As it turns out, the Amur River Line north of the Chinese border was not completed until 1916, thus providing a direct service to Vladivostok through Russian territory. Although the cost was high, this route was seen as strategically worthwhile. Revolution in China in 1911 had contributed to that Russian goal. Moreover, passing Lake Baikal by rail symbolized the power of rail to overcome geography and impose a new geometry of human creation.

The competing British rail system in Asia was very different in context and control to that of Russia. The railway route mileage of British India (which included what is now Pakistan and Myanmar) rose, thanks to private railway contractors, from 5,400 in 1872 to 25,511 in 1901 and 42,528 in 1931, the comparable figures for British-ruled Ceylon (Sri Lanka) being 70 in 1872, 297 in 1901, and 951 in 1931. The track mileage was second only to that in the United States. Economic advantage was a key element, as in the concentration of railways on the Bengal coalfield, a pattern seen across the world.

The railways the British built in India helped ensure that troops and their supplies could be moved to areas of difficulty, as in 1897 when they were sent to the North-West Frontier (of modern Pakistan) to assist in overcoming resistance among the Waziris. With railway expansion significant in the 1880s and 1890s, railheads, notably Peshawar, Quetta, and Chaman, played a key part in British planning both on that frontier and regarding power projection into neighboring Afghanistan. The ability as a result of rail to speed up deployment and improve logistics meant that there was less of a need to seek to control Afghanistan, as the buffer zone now appeared less threatening. In turn, these railheads and the routes from them had to be protected, while an anxious eye was kept on the development of the rival Russian rail network into Central Asia.

There was also growing British anxiety about Germany as it developed a *Weltpolitik*. In part, this was a matter of challenging Britain at sea in a "naval race," but there was also a German commitment to rail-based geopolitics. This involved the development of colonies, notably in Africa, for example, Cameroon, with rail serving as a way to support advances into the interior and the resulting economic exploitation.

There was also an interest in using rail to enable Germany to breach any geographical attempt to limit it on land to Europe. Breaking out entailed rail links from Germany via its leading ally, Austria, into the Balkans and thence the use of rail to benefit from the geopolitical possibilities offered by the far-flung Turkish Empire. This became more significant once Germany failed to beat Britain in the naval race, a failure that was apparent by 1909. In this sense, the Mackinder approach of a focus on Continental rail links appeared to have greater salience.

In 1888, the first train from Austria reached Constantinople (modern Istanbul), the capital of the Turkish Empire. This led to interest in moving further east, the Germans finishing a line from the eastern side of the Bosporus across western Anatolia to Ankara in 1892. The British in turn, having themselves dropped the idea, sought to thwart plans to develop a rail route through the Turkish Empire to the Persian Gulf, not least by persuading Kuwait not to be a terminus: in 1897, when the Shaikh of Kuwait was assassinated by his half brother, Mubarak, the latter won British naval support against his Turkish overlords. As a result, in 1899, Mubarak agreed not to receive foreign agents or cede land without British permission. However, instead, in 1899 a German company was granted a Turkish concession to build a line to the Turkish-ruled port of Basra on the Persian Gulf.

David Fraser, a special correspondent for the *Times*, having traveled along the Asian route of the projected Berlin-to-Baghdad Railway in 1908, apparently another

Trans-Siberian, was in no doubt in his book *The Short Cut to India* (1909) that, although very expensive for both Germany and Turkey, the railway represented a threat to Britain: "A great rival is penetrating into our commercial preserves, and establishing himself over against a possession which all the world envies us," a reference to India. Fraser saw the motivation as strategic, not economic: "Our trade [to the Gulf] is unlikely to be affected by an enterprise from which economic results are not expected." He argued, however, that the project would hit British prestige and influence and added that it would be worrying if the railway fell under Germany or a hostile Russia: "We might very well wake one morning to find that Russia has bought the Baghdad Railway and intended linking it up with her Trans-Caucasian system. A remote contingency, no doubt, but one which not so very long ago was regarded as worth discussion in political circles in Europe. The very thought of it smells of war." A German military mission arrived in Turkey in 1913, and German influence grew such that, in August 1914, the two negotiated an alliance. Nevertheless, that June, Germany was willing to agree with Britain not to extend the line south of Baghdad to Basra. In practice, war intervened, but the strategic importance of the Berlin–Baghdad railway had been greatly exaggerated by both sides.

The Turkish Empire was not only subject to the rail plans of others but also a player in its own right, and more so than China. The Hejaz Railway was long projected with army support as a means to strengthen the position of the empire in its distant Arabian dominions, and with a planned extension from Medina to the Yemeni centers of Hodeida, Sana, and Tais. Turkish suzerainty had been recently reestablished in Yemen, with Sana captured in 1872. However, a Yemeni rebellion in 1876 was only suppressed with difficulty, and there was an even more serious one in 1904–11. A railway would permit the deployment of forces without needing to rely on Red Sea routes, which were under effective British control after the establishment of British control in Egypt in 1882 and the consequent British dominance of the Suez Canal and naval base at Alexandria. Beginning in 1839, there was also a British base at Aden. The establishment of Italy in Eritrea, with a naval base at Massawa from 1885 on, underlined this issue, and in 1911, during the Italian-Turkish war, the Italians attacked Red Sea ports in Arabia, following in 1912 with completely destroying the Turkish Red Sea squadron in the Battle of Kunfuda Bay on the Arabian coast.

Separately, the Italians constructed a railway from Massawa to the main inland city of Asmara, but, begun in 1887, that was opened only in 1911, being extended to Keren in 1922 and Bishia in 1932. It was similar to the standard coast-to-interior pattern of railways in Africa.

As a reminder of the varied bases and expressions of geopolitics, the Hejaz Railway was seen in part as a way to help pilgrims to Mecca and thus to demonstrate the religious credentials of the ruling dynasty. Begun in 1900, the 1,320 kilometer (820 mile) narrow gauge railway, which also had a branch from Syria via Haifa to the port of Acre, was opened in 1908.

As a reminder of the range of geopolitics that was at play, the local Arab tribes, which saw their autonomy and their interests threatened, were hostile, which helped ensure that the railway terminated at Medina and not, as originally intended, Mecca. This change was a classic instance of the gap between plans and achievements that was so important to geopolitical planning. Stopping at Medina could be seen as affecting the Turks' ability to consolidate their position in Yemen and to threaten the British colony in Aden to the south, but it was a rational response to the difficulties facing the project.

Attacked and damaged during World War I, most famously by T. E. Lawrence (Lawrence of Arabia) as the adviser of British-backed Arab insurgents, the track saw insufficient maintenance during the conflict, a particular problem in the heat of the region. A victim also of the postwar division of the Turkish Empire between a number of states, including British control in Jordan and Palestine (later Israel) and French in Syria and Lebanon, much of the Hejaz line was disused by 1922, with the section in modern Saudi Arabia not used since 1920.

Mackinder's rail-focused ideas paralleled those pursued in Germany, notably by Otto von Bismarck, for good relations with Russia, a stance abandoned under Wilhelm II, who, in contrast, was also more interested in a naval buildup. Indeed, it is important to remember that, whatever Mackinder's argument, there were also commentators emphasizing naval themes, notably the American Alfred Thayer Mahan, author of *The Influence of Sea Power upon History, 1660–1783* (1890), and the Briton Julian Corbett, author of *Some Principles of Maritime Strategy* (1911).[20] While not formally engaging in the language of geopolitics, these were books and other writings that in practice were suffused with a maritime geopolitics.

Indeed, that was also the case with Mackinder as he thought about how best to respond to the threatening developments in Eurasia. Like other British politicians of the period, Mackinder sought imperial cooperation, naval buildup, domestic cohesion, organizational reform, and national renewal, a theme that seemed real and relevant but also involved the perception that was so significant to the international relations of these years.[21] Geopolitics, for him and others, was not solely a matter of power-political international competition.

—॥॥—

TWO

FROM WORLD WAR I TO
ITS SEQUEL, 1914–39

THE GEOPOLITICS OF RAIL PREDICTED prior to World War I were not to the fore during the conflict. For example, the Berlin–Baghdad line was both incomplete and not able to determine strategy or operations, although it was important in helping in the movement of Turkish troops and supplies. This was particularly so as Turkey had scant road transport. Rather than transcontinental lines, it was domestic systems that were of greatest significance, as they made it possible to mobilize the economic potential of the combatants. Rail also underlined the significance of Germany's position, for the conquest of Serbia in 1915, of most of Romania in 1916, and of much of western Russia in 1915–18, by Germany and its allies, Austria and Bulgaria, helped produce a rail-linked bloc of territory. The occupation of Romania in 1916 and of much of Russia in 1917–18 provided direct control over raw materials.[1] The movement west of resources, notably food, from these new conquests gave Germany great potential, not least to offset the highly damaging British-organized blockade. Yet, as it turned out, the oceanic transport systems that provided both articulation for the British formal and informal empires and the means to deploy US resources to Europe proved more significant to eventual Allied victory.

More specifically, the geopolitics underlying German policy in 1914 proved flawed. Concern about a Russian threat and the wish to see a war that would weaken Russia before it became too strong proved misplaced. The Russian offensive against Germany failed in 1914, Germany conquered Russian Poland in 1915, in 1917 two revolutions greatly weakened Russia, and in 1918 it accepted terms that left Germany dominant and able to transfer forces westward. All this had been achieved at a relatively modest cost compared to the much greater effort required for unsuccessful war with the Western powers in 1914–18 and with the Soviet Union in 1941–45.

The geopolitics that influenced the German General Staff, supposedly the most effective army planners of the period, were crude, poorly conceived, inadequately executed, and a curious hodgepodge of detailed operational planning and flawed strategic assumptions. Thus, in 1914 and 1917 the costs of bringing Britain and the United States, respectively, into the war were discounted in the furtherance of bold planning to knock France and Britain, respectively, out of the war. In contrast, strategy and operational planning were more closely in alignment for Britain and France.

As with so much else, World War I provided transformative opportunities. Indeed, the possibility offered by German-Soviet alignment, however forced, as in 1918, was one that was of significance thereafter with links between the two powers in the 1920s and an alliance from August 1939 to June 1941. The last was strongly supported by

Germany's leading geopolitician, Karl Haushofer (1869–1946). He believed that such an alliance offered Germany security from a two-front war, its unwanted fate in World War I, as well as access to vast natural resources, spatial mass, and an alliance against Britain.

Encouraged in part by German intervention in 1917, the Russian Revolution had been followed by foreign intervention that did not include Germany in the subsequent Russian Civil War. Having failed with what would later be termed "rollback," the opponents of the Soviet Union then turned to what would be called "containment." This entailed supporting governments hostile to the Soviets, notably in Eastern Europe, opposing Soviet influence in other states (Iran, Afghanistan, China) and resisting what was presented, with much reason, as subversion, both in imperial metropoles and in colonies. Communist doctrine presented subversion and propaganda, as an aspect of what is now termed "hybrid warfare," on a continuum with guerrilla warfare and full-scale conflict. The Soviet Union, its supporters, and its allies were contained, notably in 1919–29 in Hungary, Poland, and China and in 1929–38 in China and Spain.

Communist expansionism, however, conceived and in part exaggerated, was part of a sense of a dramatically different geopolitical situation after World War I. The axes of Russian/Soviet interest might be presented as similar, but a new geopolitics was offered by the Soviet capacity to pursue support and takeover by revolutionary means.

This was an aspect of the geopolitical flux of 1917–23, one that saw major changes in political systems, international engagement, and territorial control. Much related to the likely terms of the US engagement with world politics and, more specifically, Europe, for a new prospect had been set in motion by the American entry into World War I in 1917, its most significant hitherto in international relations. However, subsequently, US membership in the League of Nations was not brought to fruition as President Woodrow Wilson intended.

So also with Mackinder trying to develop his prewar ideas. In his *Democratic Ideals and Reality. A Study in the Politics of Reconstruction* (1919), he suggested joint Anglo-American trusteeship over the key naval positions of Singapore, Aden, Suez, Malta, Gibraltar, and Panama to assure the "peace of the ocean." Such notions were fanciful. To argue that there were later to be elements of such cooperation during the Cold War and that Mackinder was therefore prescient is to neglect the vital level of context. In 1919, Mackinder was clutching at straws more than offering an effective guide to policy. The Washington Naval Treaty was a more realistic outcome, as, in accepting naval parity between the new powers, Britain helped manage a transition. It voluntarily relinquished its traditional superiority at sea, while maintaining sufficient naval strength to protect its vital interests.[2]

Haushofer was to think the invasion of the Soviet Union in 1941 a major mistake. To Hitler, however, the invasion was necessary and inevitable in order to bring his race geopolitics to fruition. Indeed, race-based theses of nationalism essentially looked to race geopolitics, although not with the genocidal drive and consequences of Nazi policies.

There was also an economic dimension, one again that reflected the zero-sum suppositions that for many influenced their geopolitical assumptions. Centralized planning and protectionism contributed to this situation. In the case of Nazi Germany, the economy of Europe, both conquered and allied, was to be made subservient to German interests, as with the additional geoeconomic rationale for German intervention in the Spanish Civil War.[3] This included the provision of forced labor, whether transferred to Germany or controlled in place, as well as raw materials and food, and the receipt in return of German industrial products on German terms. Currency rates were to be controlled to facilitate the operation of this system to Germany's benefit.

The technological background was changing rapidly. The capacity for mobility and tactical advantage offered by air power ensured that it was increasingly seen as a major strategic asset and one that offered a new approach to geopolitics, with geopolitical considerations encouraging the development of air services to link imperial possessions, notably by the British to Hong Kong, Australia, and South Africa. Imperial Airways, a company founded with government support in 1924, pioneered new routes and services. This prefigured the American case after World War II. The same was true of the Dutch Empire: beginning in 1930, there was a weekly service between Amsterdam and Batavia (modern Jakarta), the capital of the Dutch East Indies. French airlines crossed the Sahara en route to French West Africa. Air power was seen as a fusion of control with modernization.[4]

The military dimension was clear. In 1935–36, in a crisis in relations between Britain and Italy, the Mediterranean fleet was withdrawn from Malta to Alexandria due to fear of Italian air attack. Territory appeared to fall victim to range, as in the name of the prototype for the German long-range bomber that was not, as it turns out, brought to fruition, the "Ural." By the end of 1935, the Soviets had a 170-strong bomber force able to reach Japan and to threaten Japanese communications with Manchuria. The significance of territorial control appeared to change, with a stronger emphasis on the value of strategic bombing as a way to destroy the opposing economy and demoralize its population, thus avoiding the need to break through the front line. In Britain, bombing was seen as a way to avoid a military commitment to continental Europe and the political entanglements to which this would give rise. In 1936, when he resigned as chief of the (British) Imperial General Staff, Sir Archibald Montgomery-Massingberd, very much an army man, wrote: "I feel that the biggest battle that I have had to fight in the last three years is against the idea that on account of the arrival of air forces as a new arm, the Low Countries [Belgium, Netherlands] are of little value to us and that, therefore, we need not maintain a military force to assist in holding them.... The elimination of any commitment on the Continent sounds such a comfortable and cheap policy ... especially among the air mad."[5]

In turn, the geopolitical problems facing Britain in the 1930s prefigure those that the United States has encountered in the early decades of the twenty-first century and that China might confront in the future. More specifically, there was the need to determine the existence, severity, promptness, and linkages of threats. For the latter, there was the question of capability as opposed to intention but also the extent to which threats might be brought to the fore in severity, timing, and linkages depending on the response. Confusing the situation was the degree to which public commentators were apt to adopt partisan positions and, as was normal, ones advanced with complete conviction. Alongside this came the fiscal, economic, and administrative challenges of affording, constructing, and sustaining forces. The changing strategic landscape was also significant, as the rise of Japan meant that naval rivals could not be locked up in Europe as had been the policy hitherto followed by Britain. In turn, it was necessary to plan for conflict across great distances, which posed operating problems for all services. There were also the issues of force prioritization in the face of threats. This was notably so if there was an awareness of a degree of obsolescence in response to changes in opposing forces, for example, of Britain's Mediterranean defenses in the face of naval and air developments.[6]

In the case of Britain in the 1930s, there were not only the external threats posed by Germany, Italy, Japan, and the Soviet Union but also rebelliousness within the empire, notably on the North-West Frontier of British India and in Palestine. There might be an apparent clarity of resolve abroad helping lead to stability in the empire, but there was no necessary relationship. Indeed, in 1916, rebellion in Ireland and, more seriously, in 1917 in Russia had come to the fore thanks in part to German assistance. The discussions of the Chiefs of Staff and the cabinet saw the difficulties of assessment in the face of threats. There was much use of geostrategic assessment, for example, in the development of the Singapore naval base in order to support a forward deployment of naval units against Japan and thus protect interests in the Far East. In geopolitical terms, this strategy was important to imperial cohesion in that it provided coverage for Australasia, but it did not lead to joint action with the United States against Japan and thus protect interests in the Far East until that was provoked by Japanese aggression. In the event, the battle of the Java Sea in 1942 saw total Japanese victory, and thereafter, there was no real cooperation until 1945. In execution, the idea of the Singapore strategy proved a total failure. With Germany, the British focus, instead, was more on air power, and geographical issues of range were to the fore. A lack of clarity over challenges, and therefore objectives other than in a general fashion, characterized not only British policy but also attempts to align with allies.[7]

In the 1930s, there was no geopolitical compulsion about the policies and strategies of other powers. Japan, for example, had policymakers, such as General Kazushige Ugaki, minister of war during 1924–27 and 1929–31, who focused on the Soviet threat, while others were more concerned about China. In turn, the latter concern was in part a matter of China as a potential Soviet ally or diversionary second front or as a useful resource area. In terms of Mackinder-based analysis, this concern could be seen as one between "heartland" and "rimland," with the Japanese position in China as an instance of the expansion of the latter. Yōsuke Matsuoka, a foreign office official and later president of the South Manchurian Railway Company, before being Japanese foreign minister in 1940–41, saw alliance with Germany and Italy as a balance to the US. He also pressed for a Japanese attack on Siberia in 1941.

France also adapted to enmities. Having competed with Italy in the 1920s and responded in particular to the Italo-Spanish alignment, France refocused on Germany. France's strategic situation posed major problems. It was dependent on transporting troops from North Africa and drew most of its oil supplies from the Caribbean. This entailed concern about the security of the Mediterranean and the North Atlantic.

For the United States over the first two decades of the twenty-first century, the focus on a particular challenge such as China similarly provides a way to deal with issues of prioritization. It is inherently logical but also risks downplaying other challenges, for example, from North Korea. The idea that China can control the latter today is questionable.

Geopolitical ideas were particularly influential in the 1930s, including in would-be great powers, such as Italy in Africa and the Mediterranean. Geopolitical ideas were particularly apparent as imperial powers, such as France, the Netherlands, and Belgium, sought to explain, justify, and develop their colonial inheritances.

The nature of rhetoric, context, and constraints of logistics and the identification of national interests in part in terms of the character of a system played a role in the retrospective definition of such interests offered in 1944 by Viscount Maugham, a cabinet minister in 1938–39, in *The Truth about the Munich Crisis*, an appeal for a geopolitics of caution and realism:

> It is always easy to write a vigorous article or to deliver an eloquent oration denouncing oppression and cruelty by any state however remote and urge on our Government—which will of course be described as pusillanimous—acts which must lead to war. . . .
>
> Nothing is so foolish as the idea that Great Britain can or should act as the schoolmaster of the world. There are remote countries where we could not launch and maintain

a large expedition against a well-armed enemy with any real hope of success for the reason, amongst others, that supplies on the scale required by modern mechanised war would be impossible. The magnitude of the problem has greatly increased since the last war. The supplies of petrol, mines, shells, spare parts, food, and of all the multifarious planes, tanks, guns, carriers, and other mechanical vehicles, and repair outfits, call for an enormous quantity of shipping facilities, and a use of roads and railways which may be the objects of continuous attack by air.

It should be admitted that the interests of Great Britain may be indirectly involved if the enemy is engaged in acts of aggression against another country which seem to form part of a system which will sooner or later bring him into an attack on Britain or its interests. This is perhaps only expressing in a more modern form the proposition that we are interested in seeing that the Concert of Europe is not seriously disturbed.[8]

Such views might have been valid in 1938, but by 1944 the Americans were contemplating a bolder assessment of interest in a global new order.

—w—

US APPROACHES TO GLOBAL STRUGGLE

"IF JAPAN AND GERMANY ARE allowed to join hands in India, the Axis will have the advantages of 'the inner line'—on a world scale. Uninterrupted Axis control of Eurasia's huge masses, from Le Havre to Shanghai, would transform the New World into an island and the two surrounding oceans into highways of invasion." The text accompanying Richard Edes Harrison's "One World, One War," published in *Fortune* in March 1943, supported the interventionism that was then central to US policy. Apparently, the fate of India would determine whether Germany and Japan could invade the United States. Liberal interventionism, the active military side of liberal universalism, rested in large part on defense in response to a sense of threat and, specifically, the thesis that this could not be provided by the apparent alternative of a "hemispheric defense" stance of dominance of the Americas and the protection of ocean shores alone. The latter stance was a key element in isolationist arguments.

These arguments drew on short-term strands in US political culture and on a longer wariness about the domestic

consequences of globalism. These consequences reach
to the present, notably in a potent nativism. At the same
time, for many American commentators, it was the sense
of national power that was a key element and the degree
to which this illuminated discussion of roles and conjunctures.[1] This sense both contributed to the Spanish-
American War of 1898 and stemmed from it. As a result
of the war, the United States conquered the Philippines
and became a Pacific power, as pointed out by Mahan in
The Problem of Asia (1900).

In its early decades, US assertiveness, both in the
struggle for independence and in the War of 1812–15
with Britain, owed much to the rivalry of France with
Britain, a rivalry that provided the United States with
opportunities for successful action. In turn, from 1815
on, hemispheric expansion benefited from an absence
of competitiveness on the part of a Britain that had con-
clusively beaten France and was thereafter unwilling to
assist Spain, Mexico, and Native Americans. This also ensured that the United States could wage a bitter civil war
in 1861–65 without external intervention, unlike China
in the same period. Dominant in its own area, the US
could then develop a transoceanic assertiveness that fed
into a growing sense of power. That was an equivalent to
the timing of British ideas of a Greater Britain imperial
federalism, but in the case of the United States, there
was not an equivalent concern about a challenge from
rising powers. This concern did not really develop in the
US case until later, first with a fear of Axis expansionism
in the early 1940s, then with the atomic risk of the Cold
War, and, in the twenty-first century, with the emergence
of China as a potent rival.

US globalism did not need air power, however much the latter gave it new force. Indeed, this globalism dated more from the period of Mackinder's lecture, although his concern was primarily with Russia, which, despite its buildup of a large fleet, did not pose a naval challenge of any significance to Britain. The US war with Spain in 1898 was both product and cause of a geopolitics that drew on a range of concerns and interests. The most long-lasting was that of hemisphere concern, one seen with the Monroe Doctrine in 1823 and taken forward, first, with US interventions in Latin America and, then, with the pressure on other European powers not to do likewise, notably Britain and Germany over Venezuela. The war with Spain was a culmination as it arose over Cuba, an island of long-standing US interest. Indeed, in the mid-nineteenth century, there had been calls to annex Cuba. The war proved a prelude to fresh interventions in Cuba, notably in 1912 to protect US property, as well as to the building of the Panama Canal, finished in 1914 and accompanied by a US occupation zone, the purchase of the Danish Virgin Islands in 1917, and interventions in Haiti, the Dominican Republic, and Nicaragua.

US geopolitics in Latin America had changed greatly from those of the mid-nineteenth century. Most obviously, the United States no longer sought to annex Mexican territory but, instead, gained access to the Mexican market. The United States eventually controlled all the major extractive industries there. The geostrategic struggle for territorial control in North America had evolved into a geoeconomic struggle for markets, one that the United States was increasingly to conduct not only in Latin America and East Asia but on a world scale.

In the second half of the nineteenth century, there was a significant extension of US military, political, and economic interests across the Pacific, with the deployment of a squadron to Japanese waters in 1853–54 to "open up" the country a key episode. A series of acquisitions, notably Hawaii, the Philippines, Guam, and Samoa, testified to this interest. They supported US political and economic roles in the western Pacific and East Asia, particularly China, Korea, and Japan. These roles interacted with the interventionism of other Western powers, particularly Britain and Russia, as well as with the China crisis that came to the fore in the mid-nineteenth century and proved a focus of geopolitical instability until the 1950s. This crisis owed much to internal tensions, as seen initially with the unsuccessful Taiping Rebellion of 1850–64, but the international interventions of that period, especially war with Britain and France in 1856–60 and the Russian seizure of territory in 1858–60, were major elements. Geopolitical analysis would put a focus on the latter, but it was of consequence in large part due to the persistent domestic turmoil within China that culminated in 1949–50 with the consolidation of Communist control there, including Hainan and Tibet but not in Taiwan. The immediate crisis then spilled over into Chinese intervention in 1950 in the Korean Civil War, which in Communist terms was in part designed to stop the United States from using Korea as a base from which to launch counterrevolution in China. That Korea was also an aspect of US containment strategy underlined the point about geopolitics being about perception as much as geography.

Beginning in the 1890s, the US naval drive had acquired a mass of its own irrespective of particular requirements.

Thus, by 1910, the United States had the third largest number of capital ships in the world, after Britain and Germany, but ahead of France. What this meant in terms of geopolitics was not immediately clear. Having beaten Spain easily in 1898, the United States acquired the means to do so again more easily, but there was no such need, and Britain, the obvious military rival, was no longer a political competitor. There was a contrast with the German drive for naval strength. Indeed, US geopolitics was to be started anew in 1917 by the need to react to a wartime German unilateral navalism that was aimed against Britain, not the United States. The force structure of the US Navy might appear in 1917 to 1918 to be poor, overly focused on capital ships and not antisubmarine capabilities.[2] That point, however, underlines the difficulties of relating, let alone aligning, force development, strategy, policy, and geopolitics. Antisubmarine capabilities were certainly necessary in 1917, but US battleships were also a guarantor against the danger of a future Jutland leading to heavy British battleship losses.

In turn, liberal universalism had been widely discredited in the United States by the reaction against President Woodrow Wilson's intervention in World War I in 1917 and his subsequent plans for a League of Nations as part of the ambitious peace settlement. As a related but also distinct process, this settlement included not only naval disarmament for Germany but also, separately, the attempt to fix the sizes and ratios of naval strength to ensure no more naval races. The US played a major role in 1921–22, with Washington the site of the key conference. This process, which was not disarmament but rather consolidation, had significant geopolitical consequences, notably in terms of potential naval strength both overall and in particular oceans. As such, the process is a reminder that geopolitics had many rooms in its mansion and, if few owners in formal, explicit, theoretical terms, nevertheless many who were involved.

Indeed, a very different geopolitics was to the fore during the Republican administrations of 1921–33, not least a xenophobia seen in concerns about international left-wing tendencies and in moves to limit immigration. The former concerns looked toward the development of the national security state, notably the establishment of the Federal Bureau of Investigation (FBI).[3] Moves to limit immigration were an important aspect of geopolitics that tend to be underplayed by the standard emphasis on geopolitics as territory. Instead, the geopolitics of migration are an important issue, with, indeed, immigration measures a key aspect of this territorial control and one that became more significant beginning in the 1870s, in part leading to a segmentation of migration systems.[4] Much conventional discussion of geopolitics is apt to downplay, if not ignore, immigration, a "top-down" approach that fails to capture the significance of population flows. Another aspect of the demographics of geopolitics was provided by the classification of population, through categorization, censuses, notions of inferior races, eugenicist ideas, and the politics of birth control.[5]

From a very different direction, German geopolitics in the 1920s also entailed a concern with population, although not with migration. In this case, the emphasis was on Germans living outside Germany, this being a geopolitics of purpose through victimhood. In turn, this was transformed into a justification for ethnic redistribution and then genocidal warfare that became a key aspect of geopolitics. Prior to World War I, there had already been much interest in ethnic and religious violence, including expulsion, and this had become more pronounced during the conflicts of the 1910s, first the Balkan Wars of 1912–13, then World War I, and, finally, the subsequent warfare that closed with the Greek-Turkish settlement of 1923. Large-scale ethnic intimidation, violence, movements, and expulsion became a significant aspect in the conceptualization and practice of geopolitics.

Indeed, taking population out of geopolitics is a fundamental mistake and never more so than when considering German strategy during World War II. The argument that there were illogical choices, notably using resources for the Holocaust that should have been employed for the war effort, particularly rail capacity, or so mistreating Soviet laborers that large numbers were killed, ignores the degree to which race conflict was central to a geopolitics of German sway, especially, but not only, over Eastern Europe. This was seen across the range of attitudes, policies, and practices, including the contrast between occupation in Western and Eastern Europe. Partisan activity contributed to the sense of the alien character of the occupied territories, but this was most apparent in European Europe due to racial attitudes. Rather than partisan activity being responsible for harsh rule there, the Germans, from the outset, had a set of beliefs, attitudes, and policies that contributed greatly. There was a top-down character to this geopolitics, one that reflected Nazi ideology and policy. At the same time, these attitudes were widely held and only in part due to incessant propaganda. As a consequence, the army's extensive involvement in the geopolitics of Nazi violence was not simply due to its own counterinsurgency tradition nor to utilitarian considerations.[6]

The relationship between territory and people could be important in turning the output of conquest or alliance into the outcome of cooperation. Neither Germany nor Japan turned out to do so well. Indeed, their rhetorics, whether anti-Communism and antisemitism in the first case or anticolonialism in the second, proved somewhat ineffective, and that despite an initial tide of military success and the popularity of some of what they had to offer. The interplay of cooperation, resistance, and the in-between was a sphere that the Germans could seek to direct but that was also impervious to a degree to German control. As a result, the Germans did not get the utility they needed from their allies and conquests.[7]

There was also a cultural dimension. The Nazis aimed to supplant France in European cultural life and to confront Anglo-American modernity in creating a German-dominated European culture. However, these ends clashed with individual national perspectives before succumbing to the failure of German war making.[8] Aside from the problems of eliciting cooperation, the Germans lacked an efficiency comparable to US capitalism. Allied attack, notably bombing and blockade, increased the problems of winning co-operation but did not inherently create them.

The idea of a regional bloc under Japanese leadership was expressed in terms of the Greater East Asia Co-Prosperity Sphere. This had a modernizing and "Greater Asianism" dimension, as well as the Japanese interest in resources that led to insistence on direct control over the Dutch East Indies. Furthermore, the competitive dimension of international relations meant that the "sphere" was also a geopolitical negativity in the sense of being intended to prevent other powers from threatening Japan or thwarting its intentions, most notably by supplying opposition in China.

In practice, there was an inchoate dimension to the implementation of Japanese geopolitical aspirations. As with Germany, there were differences with allied nationalists, especially in China. There was also an improvised character in the Japanese political arrangements in their sphere, while the whole was affected by the strains of campaigning, resource allocation, and the growing lack of success.[9]

A different geopolitics was at stake in the revival of US internationalism. It essentially came in 1940, provoked by the fears aroused by the German takeover of the European Atlantic coast from the Northern Cape to the Pyrenees and by the apparent imminence of the fall of Britain. The United States therefore would be unable to see the Atlantic as a benign space. This led to a rapid US military buildup, especially of the navy, and to the provision of supplies to Britain (notably through lend-lease), which was a key extension of geopolitical commitment.

In large part, such supplies were an aspect of the "forward buffer" nature of geopolitics, one seen in the twenty-first century with the US provision of aid to Ukraine and Taiwan. Such a stance can risk limiting geopolitical options for the aiding power, as has happened to the United States in the Middle East since the 1960s with its assistance to Israel.

In the case of 1940, anxiety turning to fear played a major role in the response to German and Japanese success. In practice, Hitler remained focused on Europe, and the Japanese in China, but there was still the danger that their success would lead to oceanic adventurism and expansionism. Indeed, should it occur, taking control over the possessions of Denmark, the Netherlands, France, and Britain would provide Germany with a series of Atlantic bases and Japan the same for the Pacific. This was a dynamic situation, as shown in particular by the fate of Iceland, where British action precluded that by Germany.

There was also propaganda emphasizing the necessity to be forward acting to ensure security. Henry Luce, the publisher of *Time*, *Life*, and *Fortune* magazines, offered warnings supported by maps by the innovative cartographer Richard Edes Harrison. His *Three Approaches to the U.S.* illustrated an article in *Fortune* in September 1940 about the readiness of the US military, asking: "Our line of minimum physical security stretches from Alaska to the Galapagos, from Greenland to the Amazon Valley. Have we the 'with what' to hold it?"

In practice, the suggestions in this article and in many other geopolitical speculations were somewhat fanciful, for cartography can lead to the abandonment of prudential considerations such as scale, terrain, and other aspects of feasibility. The map of the "From Berlin" approach was somewhat extraordinary, the accompanying text declaring: "A great-circle route from Berlin here passes through Detroit. The fanciful can see, if they wish, a pincers movement extending from Newfoundland down the New England coast and down the St Lawrence to the continent's heart; a third arm reaching to the south shore of Hudson Bay, where the terrain permits quick construction of landing fields. And there is no east-west highway north of the Great Lakes."

The approach "From Tokyo" foregrounded Alaska, adding text in which, instead of determinism, distance was discussed in terms of attitudes and human responses: "The direct line from most Asiatic ports approaches the U.S. from this angle. The coastal valleys seem temptingly remote from the U.S. center of population, 2,000 miles away across mountains, Badlands, and plains. But the map does not reckon with a transportation system that could put a fully equipped army of half a million men into Seattle in a matter of days—if we had the army." There was no mention of the point that Japan, while able to threaten the Aleutians and Hawaii, lacked the "lift" and logistical system to transport a large army to the continental United States. Japan was far more of a threat in this respect than North Vietnam during the Vietnam War, but there were still major issues of practicality.

This point is more generally true of much geopolitical discussion. Logistics is a major problem for the deployment and projection of power, one that has been consistently underplayed, not least with Mackinder's confidence about the relative ease with which rail could link the parts of Eurasia.

Harrison's map "From Caracas" was more menacing as it more readily presented much of the United States. The text brought in economics: "If an enemy should ever establish himself on the northern shore of South America or in the mazes of the West Indies, he would cut first at the US G-string the [Panama] Canal, then rip at the soft belly here displayed. For the Gulf Coast—with oil, salt, sulfur, coal, and gas—is becoming a great chemical stewpot nourishing, shaping, and extending industry, a modern analogue to the earlier iron-ore economy of the Great Lakes."

In practice, the plans of the German *Kriegsmarine* focused on a transatlantic attack using Spanish and Portuguese island territories, the Canaries and the Azores, as bases, drawing for this on the support of their right-wing regimes. Moreover, the theme of target selection as a motivator for strategy and director of geopolitics ensured that Chesapeake Bay, with the Atlantic fleet base at Norfolk, appeared the prime target for the Germans. Focused on Britain, but with an obvious relevance for the United States, the *Kriegsmarine's* plans in 1938 and 1940 replaced the limited one of 1934, which had been directed essentially against France. Instead, in a clear pursuit of a naval *weltpolitik* very different to that for a European heartland, more ambitious interest in a strong surface navy with a global reach included Atlantic bases from which it would be possible to threaten the convoy routes that brought Britain crucial supplies, as well as greater German influence in South America.

Hitler certainly wanted to regain the African colonies lost in World War I, but that was an instance of geopolitics as revenge rather than as a geographical placement. Indeed, there was no geostrategic rationale to regaining Togo, Cameroon, South-West Africa, and Tanganyika: the geopolitics was very different. In demographic terms, there was no similarity to revanchist plans for Eastern Europe. Moreover, for Hitler, regaining these overseas colonies was very much tangential to his central concern with reversing the Versailles peace settlement in Europe as the basis for creating a new Europe. Separately, the Kriegsmarine was not central to his goals, while its interest in the establishment of bases around the Atlantic and in the Indian Ocean was scarcely credible. Whatever the role of geopolitics, however defined, the role of ideology clearly played a part in the war, as in support for the Holocaust not only in Germany but also among its allies, such as Romania.[10]

As a reminder that geopolitics as space was of scant offensive meaning without significant presence, the *Bismarck*, the most powerful German warship, sailed into the North Atlantic in May 1941 supported only by a heavy cruiser, and the *Bismarck* was sunk as a result of a massive concentration of British naval power. Subsequently, the withdrawal, in February 1942, of major German warships from Brest, the leading Atlantic base in German hands, lessened the threat posed by these warships to the Allied position in the North Atlantic and thus their potential danger as a fleet in being. The last is a geostrategic reality and thus a geopolitical prospect.

Instead, the warships were concentrated in Norwegian waters and thereby subordinated to the army's goals by being used to threaten Allied maritime shipping routes to the Soviet Union. This was a plausible goal given Anglo-American surface strength in the North Atlantic and an indication of the compromising thereby of the control of a coastline. Indeed, alongside its provision of submarine bases, the Atlantic coast of France became essentially a defensive obligation for Germany.

There was also a time sequencing to bring into the geopolitical equation. Submarine attacks require scale, method, organization, maintenance, intelligence, and luck to stand a chance in confronting antisubmarine warfare and thereby creating a blockade.[11] Moreover, as the German naval leadership appreciated, the submarine campaign was a long war tool,[12] rather like air offensives prior to the unexpected use of the atom bomb. Long war put an emphasis on energy availability, which was a key element of geopolitics, one encouraging states to try to mold circumstances that were very much spatially encoded in the sense of the location of supplies and routes, albeit with significant political and military variables.[13]

Thus, Italy was short of oil and coal and had only a limited industrial base. As a result, the geopolitical potential of an empire that included the Dodecanese, Libya, Eritrea, Ethiopia, and most of modern Somalia was far less than the map might suggest. The Italians also lacked an effective naval air arm, and their ability to challenge the Mediterranean axis of the British navy was to be dependent on the German aircraft deployed in Sicily beginning in January 1941.

As another instance of the difficulties of judging from maps, Admiral Andrew Cunningham, the able British naval commander in the Mediterranean, feared in May 1941 that the Germans might press on from capturing Crete to invade Cyprus and deploy forces in Vichy-run Syria, threatening the British position in the Middle East.[14] As it turned out, such goals were not pursued by a German military focused on the forthcoming attack on the Soviet Union.

Similarly, there was prioritization in US geopolitics, one that was not dictated by geography. Concern that Britain might collapse helped President Franklin Delano Roosevelt settle prewar in the event of war on a "Germany first" strategy focused on a US invasion of Europe. That commitment underlined the prior significance of securing the safety of Atlantic shipping lanes. This was and remains a controversial choice among US commentators, one linked to a tendency, as a result of the focus on the Japanese attack on Pearl Harbor, to forget that Germany declared war on the United States or not to treat that declaration as what amounted to a real threat. In reality, in early 1942, more German than Japanese submarines were in US coastal waters mounting attacks. Moreover, these attacks were more significant in their damage to the US war economy, notably to the coastal movement of oil. Antisubmarine warfare in the Atlantic made island bases especially important, notably those on Iceland and the Azores, the latter ending the mid-Atlantic "air gap." So also with Caribbean bases and those in Brazil.

The logic was clear: Germany, the stronger adversary and therefore with the more globally ambitious ideology, had a greater potential than Japan to overthrow its opponents, Britain and the Soviet Union, as well as to intervene in South America against US interests. In contrast, Japan was faced by the far-greater distances of the Pacific and not able to draw on an economy comparable to that of German-run Europe. The Japanese navy could only achieve so much. Although colonies, such as Malaya and the Philippines, might be conquered, Britain and the United States were far less vulnerable to Japanese power. This was crucial to US geopolitics. The central Pacific might appear close to many when Pearl Harbor was struck, but there was no sustained Japanese assault on the central Pacific, and the Philippines seemed a long way away. The panic that gripped the Californian coast at the outset of the war rapidly dissipated. Despite Japan, the United States, thanks to its geopolitical position, retained strategic choice.

FOUR

THE GLOBAL WORLD WAR II

GEOPOLITICS RESTED ON PERCEPTION AND as-
sessment, as with Hitler's rationalization of the irrational
in his decision to declare war on the United States on
December 11, 1941, a decision that moved the half war of
limits and nuance to full-scale conflict.[1] For Americans, Pearl
Harbor was also a matter of perception—"day of infamy"
and assessment. The attack demonstrated a surprising
Japanese ability to overcome the constraints of space. In
addition, there was a geographical divide in that Americans on the Pacific coast feared imminent Japanese action, which was scarcely the case on the Atlantic. This
underlines the extent to which there is a geopolitics of perception, with the related cartography of concern a matter
not only for the external features, such as coastlines, that
focused fear but also for the domestic differences over
what was feared. An extension of that, although one that
also entailed racism, was the more hostile policy adopted
to Japanese Americans than to their German and Italian
counterparts. In a particular geopolitics, there were large-
scale deportations from coastal regions.

For all states, although least for the Soviet Union, geopolitical assumptions during the war were questioned by the use of air power, which, in place of prewar speculations, posed new challenges for understanding opportunities and threats and for presenting distance, routes, and links.[2] Globes were used and referred to by some leaders, notably Roosevelt. Globes provided a clear guide to the locations of the simultaneity of conflict in the world, although not to the time-space equations. Globes also offered more than conventional accounts, although neither, at a tactical level, provided an opportunity to address the three-dimensional nature of air power and, as a related point, the three-dimensional obligations of antiaircraft weaponry and doctrine. Churchill had a well-stocked map room, with officers charged with updating them, and Hitler liked to be pictured with maps. There were very different levels of skill in the handling of the time-space equations that arose from and sustained the strategic weight of particular issues and areas, the latter two the key components of geopolitics.

Continuity was clearly at play in World War II geopolitics, with many who were prominent having also been so during World War I, notably Churchill, who began both conflicts as First Lord of the Admiralty. He had been in Parliament at the same time as Mackinder and in 1919–21 was secretary of state for war and air at the same time that Mackinder was a key figure in British policy in South Russia. Roosevelt had been assistant secretary of the navy from 1913 to 1920 and had great interest in the works of Alfred Thayer Mahan.

The public requirements for propaganda and public education were apparent but addressed more effectively by some commentators. Thus, centered on the North Pole, Harrison's "The World Divided," published in *Fortune* in July 1941, carried a note explaining the north polar azimuthal equidistant projection used: "The World Centrifuged . . . The principle of this projection may be illustrated by a dancer with a skirt in the shape of a globe upon which is inscribed the map of the world. When she whirls the skirt rises to a horizontal plane and the map on it will then resemble the map on this page. The projection has two important advantages: it shows little distortion of the Northern Hemisphere, and it nowhere breaks the continuity of the lands or seas involved, in the present far-flung struggle."

F. E. Manning of the *Chicago Sun* in his October 1943 "Target Berlin" and "Target Tokyo" maps, which were printed and distributed by the army, positioned the targets at the center of the map and included the explanation: "This map is a photographic view of the world with the center at Berlin. Thus, with the detachable scale, distances can be measured along any line running thru Berlin."

Manning's maps worked not only as accounts of aerial warfare but also as ways to explain the converging goal and character of Allied strategy as a whole. The idea of a target was also used by Edwin Sundberg in the *New York Sunday News* of September 3, 1944, with the map organized in terms of "bombing distances" to Tokyo marked at three-hundred-mile intervals. Indeed, air power challenged the traditional geopolitical dichotomy of land and sea.[3] Writers such as Carl Schmidt in his *Land and Sea* (1942) argued that this capability of air power would revolutionize geopolitics. Air power was certainly a key threat to naval forces, both surface and submarine. In early 1942,

Admiral Sir Geoffrey Layton noted in his war diary that, in the face of the Japanese advance, "the problem of retaining control of the coastal waters of Burma was quite beyond our powers in the absence of either air superiority or fast patrol craft with good AA [antiaircraft] armament so numerous that we could afford substantial losses."[4]

The Mercator projection, in contrast, was unhelpful in the depiction of air routes: great circle routes and distances were poorly presented because distances in northern and southern latitudes were exaggerated. That projection was also criticized in print, including in *Life*, the *New York Times*, and the *Saturday Review of Literature*, as distorting the world and, in particular, exaggerating the United States' isolation from Europe.

At the same time, maps could be flawed as guides to strategy and for physical as well as political reasons. For example, in Harrison's *Look at the World: The Fortune Atlas for World Strategy* (1944), Harrison produced text for his "Four Approaches to Japan," a news map for the US armed forces published on May 8, 1944: "'Japan from Alaska' shows how the direct northern route cuts into the heart of the Japanese Empire."[5] Yet this route was greatly limited due to the problems for the United States of building up supplies in Alaska and, more generally, the issues posed by cold, ice, and the dark in winter. In cartographic terms, Alaska might be closer to Japan than was California, but the logistical possibilities of the latter were far greater for operations in the Pacific. Politically, the Alaska–Hokkaido route was not viable unless the Soviet Union cooperated, but it had a nonaggression treaty with Japan, which was not broken until August 1945. On the other hand, possibilities helped define geopolitics. Thus,

Japanese concern about a possible US threat to Hokkaido led to the stationing of significant forces there.

So also with Harrison's map "The Not-So-Soft Underside," published in *Fortune* on January 27, 1943, as Anglo-American forces prepared to battle German-Italian opponents in Tunisia, which they were successfully to do and rapidly so in a campaign in which Axis forces lost as heavily as they had recently done at Stalingrad but without the later attention. The text offered an apparent reading from the topography, which was emphasized thanks to a vertical scale that was out of proportion to that on the ground:

> No full-fledged military expedition since ancient times has succeeded in crossing the Pyrenees or the Alps from south to north and making the invasion stick. The great formative invasions since the time of the Romans have all come from east to west, from the Russian plains or the Anatolian plateau of Turkey. The "soft underside of the Axis," the "unprotected belly of Europe," is then a figure of speech that lacks geographical common sense. The mountains and sketchy roads of crippled Spain, the narrow, easily closed gap of the Rhône, the tunnels of Switzerland, the Nazi air force in Crete, pose terrifying problems of both military tactics and supply. From the communications officer's view it is thus American dollars to Italian lire that Hitler's Germany will not be invaded in force from North Africa.
>
> What did we get out of the African campaign? When the Mediterranean is cleared it will save miles of shipping. But from the positive standpoint, it spreads Hitler thin all around the margins of Europe. He must defend Italy to keep Americans from taking over airfields within easily striking distance of the Skoda works in Pilsen and Munich. . . . Possession of the Mediterranean south shore gives the United Nations the opportunity to deliver

confusing multiple blows—and Hitler's own power of the initiative has been critically impaired.[6]

Harrison's comment on the roads of a Spain much weakened by the civil war of 1936–39 captured the need to move in geopolitics from the distance and possibilities of the map to the situation on the ground. Indeed, in this map, there was an aerial perspective that was intended to provide clarity rather than to suggest an outcome for action. The idea, at the close of the quotation, that geopolitical position provided the possibility for an initiative that had value, even if not pursued, was an instructive guide to the potential of position.

In practice, however, the Allied invasion of Italy rapidly followed. The consequences of this invasion can be seen in contrasting ways. The slow pace of the advance up Italy indicated that Harrison was correct at the operational level, with the mountainous terrain and steep river valleys making movement and attack difficult. Yet, in 1943, it was hard to see how the invasion of first Sicily and then mainland Italy was not the best choice. Doing so had the benefits of increasing Allied options for maritime usage, taking specific advantage of amphibious capability, building up the relevant experience, demonstrating to the Soviet Union that the Western Allies were in land combat, weakening the Axis alliance, and increasing pressure on Germany, not least by lessening its strategic reserve. In the absence of this offensive, it is unclear that forces would have been used elsewhere in the Mediterranean with more success, and more divisions would not have greatly strengthened the Normandy operation in 1944 but would have increased the logistical burden.

The contrast between Harrison's prediction and the results suggests that whatever geography might appear to dictate, there were no necessary consequences, and notably so at the strategic level. This was very much seen with the competing agendas adopted by services and commanders, agendas for alliances as a whole, for particular states, and for individual military components. The competition between intelligence agencies compounded this situation.

Geopolitical discussion and imagery sought to offer a fixity to strategy, but in wartime, this was shown to be vulnerable to fear as the problems and results of campaigning led to pressures for changes in direction and intensity. This was seen in the Union war effort in the American Civil War in 1863. It was also seen in the war of 1944–45 as German resistance hardened, as did the use of new weapons and the prospect of more. Despair among British and US policymakers still facing the war with Japan encouraged a marked escalation of the Allied air offensive on Germany.[7] The degree to which this air offensive helped ensure no resistance after the Nazi surrender is worth speculation. Certainly, the Western Allies were not to have to devote as many forces to holding down areas over which they had advanced as the Germans had done.

World War II also saw a reconfiguration of geostrategy, first with US strategy and operational campaigning in the Pacific and then culminating with the use of atomic weaponry. The two elements were combined as the focus was on gaining Pacific islands from which Japan could be bombed. The Americans could neutralize Pacific island bases, such as Rabaul and Truk, that they chose to leapfrog. As a variant on conventional geopolitics, this was part of the more general degradation of Japanese logistics and a key aspect of their lack of strategic capability. Leapfrogging maintained the pace of the US advance, lessened the extent of hard slogging, and costly conflict by pinpointing attrition, and reflected the degree to which the Americans had and used the initiative. The last is a key element in geostrategy. Indeed, it both reflects geographical factors and yet, to a degree, can lead to them being ignored.

The full effectiveness of the combined-arms naval force was realized by combining the tools that were now in the inventory, including amphibious doctrine, carrier operations, landing craft, long-range aircraft, mobile airfield construction, and fleet supply trains. Yet geographical factors were still pertinent, including distance at the operational level. Notably so, also, at the tactical level, natural obstacles, from coral reefs to coastal cliffs to dense jungle, played a major role. Tanks could be used on relatively flat islands, such as Tinian, but less readily on others.

At the operational and tactical levels, there was a major contrast between the southwest Pacific, where the focus was on surprise landings on relatively lightly defended beaches across a range of possible targets backed by large hinterlands where substantial enemy reserves were deployed, and the central Pacific, where the Marines faced better-prepared defenses on relatively obvious targets, with less of an opportunity for surprise.

Technology was also significant in affecting geopolitics, not least the greater capacity of amphibious landing craft so that not only ports were vulnerable. The military commentator J. F. C. Fuller wrote in the *Sunday Pictorial* of October 1, 1944: "Had our sea power remained what it had been, solely a weapon to command the sea,

the garrison Germany established in France almost certainly would have proved sufficient. It was a change in the
conception of naval power which sealed the doom of that
great fortress. . . . Now ships were fitted to the invading
forces."

Political factors were also significant for geopolitical
priorities, not least prestige, an image that is generally underplayed in geopolitical analysis. Thus, the recapture of
Malaya and Singapore was regarded as very important to
British prestige in order to repair the repeated humiliating failures of imperial collapse in 1941–42. In September
1944, Admiral Sir Geoffrey Layton, commander in chief
of Ceylon, wrote of "the vital importance of our recaptur-
ing those parts of the Empire as far as possible ourselves.
I would specially mention the recapture of Burma and its
culmination in the recovery of Singapore by force of arms
and not by waiting for it to be surrendered as part of any
peace treaty . . . the immense effect this will have on our
prestige in the Far East in post-war years. This and only
this in my opinion will restore us to our former level in
the eyes of the native population in these parts." Admiral
Louis Mountbatten, the well-connected supreme commander of South-East Asia Command, strongly agreed.[8]
The views of Layton (1884–1964), a conservative who
had held a number of posts in Asian waters, reflected a
standard racist assumption about "native peoples" and
the value of the impression of success in maintaining imperial sway and geopolitical power. This assumption offered a measure of the latter that was not dependent on
formal "realist" criteria of strength, such as troop numbers. In this interpretation, battles could be decisive, as in
the Japanese victories over the Russian fleet at Tsushima

in 1905 and over the British in capturing Singapore in 1942, in that they shattered the dominant impression. As a result, strategic effect could be won by operational and indeed tactical means and with lasting geopolitical consequences.

Throughout the war, the allocation of effort, from troops to transport shipping, was important as an instance of geopolitical concern. Thus, World War II saw resource and resilience extending to geopolitical change with the establishment of important new communication links. These were varied. For Britain, there was the laying of new pipelines to move the aviation fuel that made the Combined Bomber Offensive against Germany possible. These pipelines moved fuel to the air bases in eastern England. There was also the strategic depth offered by imperial and, later, US support, including, for example, US Sherman and Grant tanks.

For the Soviet Union, there was the large-scale and rapid transplanting of industry eastward beyond the scope of German advance and air attack. This transplanting was accompanied by the construction of support networks including rail links and pipelines. This was a classic case of the acquisition, through new provision and use, of strategic depth. Initially in Leningrad, production of the KV-1 was moved east to Chelyabinsk, which became known as "Tankograd." The Kharkov tank factory moved to Nizhny Tagil, that from Kolomna to Kirov, and that from Moscow to Sveralovsk. The multifaceted Soviet defense in depth also included military reorganization and an eventual political resilience that owed much to the lack of any viable prospect for a compromise peace and any alternative to Stalin's dictatorship.

For the United States, there was the establishment of new plant, including shipyards and aircraft manufacturing, as well as the population movements that made this possible, notably to the West Coast but also from the South to manufacturing centers in the Midwest. There was also the replacement of a reliance on vulnerable coastal shipping by the Big Inch Oil Pipeline from Texas to the East Coast, a 1,254-mile pipeline built in 350 days. Constructed in 1942, the Alaska Highway was designed to provide a link able both to move troops and supplies to counter a Japanese landing and to move forward supplies for the Soviet Union that would then be taken across the Bering Strait and moved westward by the Trans-Siberian Railway. It was instructive that the Alaska route was road, not rail. The latter was more vulnerable to costly damage through permafrost and seasonal conditions affecting the route. In addition, the road could be built more rapidly. Yet a key element was the ready provision in the United States of plentiful and cheap supplies of oil.

Between the Allies, there were the geopolitics of global supply links, many new, as with those from Britain and the United States to the Soviet Union via the Arctic convoys, Iran, and the Bering Strait. One-sixth of the heavy tanks in the battle of Moscow were British, while 16 percent of the Soviet tanks on July 1, 1942, were foreign, mostly British, supplied.[9] This scarcely matched prewar geopolitical thought nor indeed its postwar counterpart. Yet the value of such deployment owed much to the intentions and moves of other powers. Thus, the Japanese determination not to anger the Soviet Union meant that the transport of US supplies on the Bering Strait route were not disrupted.

The intentions and moves of powers were not identical, as intentions could not always be realized, in part due to defensive needs. The war in the Far East in 1945 amply demonstrated this, with the Soviet Union entering the struggle with Japan only after that with Germany had finished. The latter also ensured that the United States and Britain could send more forces against Japan, but they faced war weariness. The background to the closing stages of its war for Japan was a multiple military, political, and economic failure, but Japan was still in control of much territory it had not held at the start of December 1941. The resignation of the Tojo ministry, in July 1944, one not matched in Germany, revealed a degree of realism, but the new ministry was unable to exploit this to negotiate, and a powerful fear of shame encouraged a determination to fight on. The last year of the war in the Pacific saw a narrowing of Japanese options, but the Americans faced the dilemma of how best to win in a conflict that was becoming increasingly asymmetrical without in any way ensuring US success. Moreover, the chances of an invasion of Japan succeeding without massive losses were greatly lessened by the Japanese movement of troops, notably from Hokkaido to the likely invasion island, Kyushu. This helped alter the casualty equations that affected US planning, including the use of atomic bombs. This use, the prospect of which had been highlighted in the Potsdam Conference of Allied leaders, was primarily intended to ensure Japanese surrender. The use of the atomic bombs ended differences, indeed an impasse, about what methods and goals should be applied to end the war with Japan. Moreover, these differences occurred in a context of military, political, public, and economic concerns.[10]

The case of the atomic bombs and, more generally, geopolitics also greatly affected the memorialization of the war, with postwar territorial control defining the possibilities for presentation.[11] The war was indeed to play a key role in postwar accounts. Thus, it provided vindication for the Communist government of China.[12] As such, winning this territorial control has a strategic effect at a geocultural level. More immediately, the likely geopolitical consequences of the war and the resulting territorial changes more generally were uncertain.[13]

FIVE

—◊◊◊—

THE LIBERAL
INTERNATIONALISM
OF COLD WAR US
GEOPOLITICS

SWIFTLY FOLLOWING WORLD WAR II, the Cold War between a Soviet-led alliance and a US-led one might appear to be a clear-cut case of continuity with Mackinder's 1904 perspective. In practice, there was the significant intervening stage of the earlier ideological-political contest of 1918–41 between the Soviet Union and a British anti-Communist system.

There was certainly concern about many of the same regions. Thus, beginning in 1944, the British Chiefs of Staff were actively considering postwar threats to the British world. This included concern about Soviet and, separately, Chinese Nationalist pressure on British India. For example, the Post-Hostilities Planning Staff produced a map in 1944 about projected Soviet lines of advance against India, a map that looked back to nineteenth-century anxieties. More specifically, this map was consistent with the view in British India that Baluchistan (and the Herat–Kandahar–Khojak–Bolan route) formed India's "front porch," as opposed to the route via Kabul and the Khyber Pass. To the British in 1944, western Afghanistan also formed a kind of pivot on which a Soviet force might turn toward southern Iran and, more particularly, the Strait of Hormuz bottleneck to the entrance to the Persian Gulf,[1] an area that remains of geopolitical significance to this day. So also with British anxiety about Soviet expansion into Persia (Iran), a long-standing issue that looked back to the nineteenth century, and about Soviet intervention in Chinese politics, which had been of major concern in the 1920s. As another instance of continuity, Poland had been a front line of anti-Soviet effort in 1920.

Theory also played a part. Nicholas Spykman, a Dutch immigrant who was head of the Institute for International Studies at Yale, in his *The Geography of the Peace* (1944), developed an anti-isolationist "Rimland thesis" for the United States to offset what he saw as a dangerous Soviet Union. He died, aged forty-nine, in June 1943 but was already troubled by Soviet power and the prospect of the Soviet's dominating Eastern Europe. At the same time, confident in the potential of the "rimland," Spykman emphasized the value of maritime power alongside Continental allies, the two necessary to prevent the dominance of Eurasia by any one power:

> The influence of the United States can be brought to bear on Europe and the Far East only by means of seaborne traffic and the power of the states of Eurasia can reach us effectively only over the sea. This is true in spite of the growing importance of air power because the preponderant element in the transport of all but the most specialised items will continue to be the ships that saw the oceans. . . . The United States will have to depend on her sea power communications across the Atlantic and Pacific to give her access to the Old World. The effectiveness of this access will determine

the nature of her foreign policy . . . a continental ally who can provide a base from which land power can be exercised.[2]

This, ironically, suggested a fallacy of his geopolitical argument, because the shift to air power over the next decade was to be dramatic and was to be shown over the next few decades in the aerial deployment of troops and equipment, as by the Western Allies to Berlin in 1948–49, the Soviets into Czechoslovakia in 1968, and US supplies to Israel during the Yom Kippur War in 1973. Furthermore, there was no real threat to the US position at sea until the Soviet Union built up a significant submarine force in the 1970s and 1980s.

Spykman's ideas and arguments continued to be influential beyond the Cold War. Thus, in 2022, Seth Cropsey, a former deputy undersecretary of the navy, arguing the significance of the naval dimension of the Ukraine war, wrote: "To paraphrase Nicholas Spykman's idea, Ukraine's Black Sea coast is to the Ukraine war as the rimland is to the Eurasian landmass. Control of Eurasia's coastal regions is essential to control of the interior land; so it is with Ukraine."[3]

In contrast to Spykman, Mackinder in a 1943 piece in *Foreign Affairs*, presented the Soviet Union as an ally against any German resurgence. It was an instructive aspect of the change in weight between allies that Mackinder's piece appeared in a US journal. Moreover, in terms of discussing the postwar world, it was the Americans who played a more original role than the exhausted British. In part, this contrast reflected the resources and confidence of the United States and the determination to ensure that the postwar world did not lead to an international crisis for the US comparable to that which had eventually followed World War I, a result attributed, somewhat unreasonably, to a lack of US engagement with the League of Nations, the precursor to the United Nations.

The agreements and policies of 1944–49 initiated by the United States were designed to produce a global order that would rectify the deficiencies of that after World War I.[4] As with the League of Nations, the United Nations was supposed to be a universal way to handle flaws in the peace treaties as well as to confront revisionism and new crises. Indeed, this US determination was to be transformed because the post-1945 world rapidly became far more threatening and was seen as such both in Western Europe and in the United States.

That also affected Britain although less so in some respects as there was less of an engagement there with the fate of China. In the case of Britain, the geopolitics of concern focused on imperial territories and roles, notably in the Middle East and South Asia. There was therefore a survivalist character to British geopolitics after World War II. In turn, independence for Britain's South Asian possessions in 1947–48 greatly affected these geopolitics. The nature of British imperial geopolitics changed, not least with the loss of the support of Indian manpower.

Choice was a major element at the time, choice in analysis and choice in response. Indeed, the degree to which geopolitics was a field for debate rather than a clear-cut prescription was repeatedly clear with US policy during the Cold War. This involved a whole series of choices, not least in how the world was to be visualized. This was a question not simply of which cartographic projection was to be employed but also the centering of any projection. Mackinder's generation had very much ad-opted the Greenwich meridian, but this process put the United States toward the margin. A projection centered on the US, and on the US Midwest at that, created a very different impression, as indeed remains the case. So, psy-chologically, did the view that continents were not neces-sarily the basic building blocks but, rather, oceans, as in the North Atlantic.

There was a continuity in (some) alliances and (most) bases, but not in the tasking and prioritization that are central to strategy and that provide the context for geo-politics. Indeed, largely unexpected tasks for the United States threw areas to the fore, notably South Korea begin-ning in 1950 and Israel from the late 1960s.

The usual presentation would be different, focusing not on major changes in US geopolitics but, instead, on the Cold War as the very goal and means of US policy, with ri-valry with the Soviet Union treated as geostrategic as well as ideological and grafted onto much of the assessment of earlier British policy toward, first, Russia and then the Soviet Union. Indeed, there was a continuity in the shape of the major role of Britain in the first cold war, that with Soviet Communism from 1917 to 1941. Alongside a potent ideological contrast, this role drew on the earlier British rivalry with Russia that had only ended with the entente of 1907 and then had still left a degree of mistrust and competition. Returning from Moscow in March 1946, the British diplomat Frank Roberts saw long-term geo-political factors rather than simply Communist ideology as crucial: "There is one fundamental factor affecting Soviet policy dating back to the small beginnings of the Muscovite state. This is the constant striving for security of a state with no natural frontiers and surrounded by enemies. In this all-important respect the rulers and people of Russia are united by a common fear, deeply rooted in Russian policy, which explains much of the high-handed behaviour of the Kremlin and many of the suspicions genuinely held there concerning the outside world."[5]

The Cold War would then be discussed in terms of NATO (1949) and the National Security Council's NSC 68 document (1950), and a strategic architecture based on containment would be defined. This was very different from the earlier confidence in air power that was seen immediately after World War I, a confidence that was the rationale for the establishment in 1947 of the US Air Force.[6]

Containment is very much a geopolitical concept. The United States in 1941–45 had faced a two-front war but with Germany in no real position to mount an offensive and with that from Japan largely held to the western Pacific. Beginning in 1949, the US again appeared faced by a two-front challenge, one in Europe with the Soviet Union and in East Asia with Soviet allies. The United States' alliance system and bases represented a forward commitment that had been present prior to Pearl Harbor, notably with the US position in the Philippines, but that had not been so central to US strategy. However, in 1940–41, the path to war in part was seen with US actions in response to Axis expansionism. What would happen after 1949 was unclear.

Containment as a concept that was to be applied in US policy and strategy received its intellectual rationale in a 1947 article in *Foreign Affairs* by "Mr X," George Kennan, the acting head of the US diplomatic mission in Moscow.

The emphasis on inherent Soviet antagonism under Stalin in Kennan's "long telegram" of February 22, 1946, had an impact in Washington and elsewhere and was the basis for the article. In 1947, Kennan became director of policy planning in the State Department.

The concept of containment was far from new, having been advanced in particular by the French after World War I in response to the Soviet threat to Eastern Europe, and indeed in the eighteenth century in the face of rising Russian power. Moreover, similar geopolitical attitudes and narratives provided a way to manage the transition from British leadership, notably at sea, to US predominance.[7]

With geopolitics, however, it was not novelty in conceptualization that was important but, rather, application. In this case, the key element was arguing that the United States had a major role to play in containment. In the public debate, this was accompanied by a supposed "lesson" from history—namely, that a US lack of commitment to European power politics after World War I had led to the failure to restrain Hitler that, in turn, had obliged the United States to act against Germany in World War II. As a first state, the prospect of chaos was to be limited by the offer that June of Marshall Plan aid, an economic aid policy to aid recovery. George C. Marshall, the secretary of state from 1947 to 1949, had earlier sought, in 1945–47, to mediate the Chinese Civil War, which would have brought a stabilization conducive to US interests. This was an unrealistic and futile goal, in part because countries are not readily deployed units, but nevertheless a goal that was worth trying, in part because the cost in effort was low, and there was no real alternative.

The Cold War was to be presented in large part in terms of spatial threat, notably as perceived by the Soviet Union, being surrounded by NATO and other US allies and bases. Thus, Japan resumed its role as an adjunct of the anti-"heartland" coalition, with its navy, in its focus on opposition to Soviet submarines, looking to the United States as it had at one time looked to Britain.[8]

There was also a US sense of threat in the shape of the forward projection of Soviet power, notably to Cuba in 1962 and Egypt later in the decade, but also as Soviet bases, for example in Somalia, tested any idea of containment. Thus, the Global South played a role in terms of the wider struggle. This spurred US concern about the decline of the Western European empires and the "vacuum" of power that would be followed there by the Soviet Union. The very idea of such a vacuum was inherently a spatial one focused on a specific geopolitics. The latter, in the Cold War case, also led to familiar policies, notably keeping allies aligned, enemies weak, and neutrals, such as Cambodia, cooperating.[9]

Yet what containment, and indeed the Cold War, meant for US policymakers was far from fixed. Instead, there was an essential fluidity. This extended to areas and to threats. For example, on January 5, 1957, Eisenhower announced to Congress what was to be termed the Eisenhower Doctrine, permitting the commitment of forces in the Middle East "to secure and protect the territorial integrity and political independence of such nations, requesting such aid against overt armed aggression from any nation controlled by international communism."[10] This might appear clear, but in practice the threat in the Middle East at that point was from Arab nationalism and internationalism, not from the Soviet Union. Aside from deliberate or unintentional obfuscation about the international situation, one seen later when Iraq was attacked in the post 9/11 war on terror, the fluidity in US policy in part arose from domestic political, social, and cultural pressures helping cause hostility to foreign powers that were presented as themselves linked to the internally dangerous. As a result of this situation, the Cold War has been presented as a socially constructed development.[11]

This approach underplays the real tensions at the level of the great and other powers across Eurasia, but these tensions and the apparently necessary responses in turn were perceived in a perspective of rising hostility and the related distrust. Moreover, at a functional level, much of the fluidity in perception and policy was due to the degree to which geopolitics does not occur in a one-sided perspective and on a comparable platform but, instead, involves a response to the moves of opponents and other powers.[12] The end of the Western European empires was the key element in the latter, creating, as it did, opportunities and problems aplenty as a range of new states were established. They had opportunities to maneuver both between the global blocs and in terms of pursuing regional geopolitical ambitions of their own as with Egypt, which had primacy and geopolitical interests across the Arab world.

There was optimism with decolonization, notably in the shape of growth and social and political development through modernization, whether US or Communist in its agenda. This was, as it were, an alternative theory and practice to colonialism, imperial control, and conventional geopolitics. Modernization was regarded as a form of global New Deal, able to create liberal, capitalistic, pro-US democracies.

At the same time, there were the dynamics of threat and fear for the West, and they ensured that the nature and amount of hard power that might be required to accompany international liberalism attracted attention. Thus, by 1950, the Soviet testing of atomic warheads and Mao Zedong's conquest of China in 1949 had transformed the parameters for US strategy. The preemptive action that the possibility of airborne nuclear attack appeared to make necessary[13] provided a new take on geopolitics as the space-time sequence was radically altered. In part this was a matter of the range of aircraft and the greater practicality of such attack, but alongside technology, there was also the learned experience of the damage that could be inflicted through surprise attack, in short the prospect of another Pearl Harbor. Indeed, NSC 68, the basic document of containment, was a prime instance of fear driving policy or, at least, of fear as a selling point, within government and toward the population. The Communist bloc had greatly expanded from 1939 to 1949, taking over much of Eurasia, and this posed issues of containment, deterrence, and defense.

The weakness of air power had been demonstrated in the Chinese Civil War (1946–49) when the Communists, the side that was weaker in air power, prevailed. In part, this was a reflection of specific Nationalist weaknesses, notably a lack of fuel and spare parts, and poor coordination with troops, but there was also the ability of the Communists to develop the relevant antitactics toward aerial attack. The latter was a precursor of the situation in the Vietnam War and one to which the United States devoted insufficient attention. Indeed, at the geostrategic level, the operational inability to isolate the battlefield by means of air power, one variously seen in Normandy in 1944, in Korea in 1950–53, in Cuba in 1957–58, and in Algeria in 1958–62, undercut the value of strategies proposed in terms of the mass, range, and payload of aircraft.

The issues of containment, deterrence, and defense were accentuated and brought to the fore in 1950 when, through a Soviet proxy, an attack was launched on South Korea, a state supported by the US. In response, in a classic instance of shoring up a system, one that had a political logic rather than a military one, the NATO council agreed on December 18, 1950, to a strategy of forward defense, which meant holding West Germany against Soviet attack. In turn, this commitment affected planning, deployment, and force requirements, each of which created a dynamic that helped frame a geopolitical context. In the United States, through policymaking, although not always public rhetoric, there was an understanding of the European and East Asian spheres as linked.

The need for bases was a key point, but these were now increasingly air force rather than naval, although the latter remained important, as with the continued significance of Hong Kong and Singapore to British strategy in the Far East: this was geopolitics in a traditional form.[14]

In contrast, the rail links that had interested Mackinder were not to the fore. Thus, in plans for strategic nuclear bombing, there was reliance on bases in eastern England for attacking Saint Petersburg and Moscow and in Cyprus and northern Iraq for attacking Ukraine and southern Russia. Moreover, US policy toward Spain rested heavily on a defense partnership that included air bases, under a 1953 agreement. Similarly, the role of the bases in the Azores helped to explain why Portugal, although not a democracy, was a founding member of NATO in 1949. The 1951 defense agreement with Iceland, a democratic NATO member, ensured that the United States could use the base at Keflavik, which it, in turn, paid to develop. These and British air bases were crucial both to the resupply of US forces in NATO and in providing strategic depth in the event of a Soviet advance into Western Europe that overran extensive territory.

For any such Soviet advance, and such advances were also presented in fiction, notably in John Hackett's *The Third World War* (1978), the key target was the massive Rhein-Main Air Base, just south of Frankfurt. The base was the United States' leading air transport terminal in Europe and of key significance for the US presence in West Germany. As a result, the roads focusing on Frankfurt were rapidly repaired and improved after World War II by the US occupation forces, which was an instance of the important local impact on infrastructure of air power geopolitics. The US network of bases was not restricted to NATO but also seen in Japan, the Philippines, and with the development of large aircraft carriers.

Politics was very important to this process, with reliable allies, such as Britain and Japan, providing the continuity that vindicated the geopolitics of air bases. Elsewhere, there could be difficulties. Thus, for the Western European empires, the retreat of imperial power and the provision of aircraft to independent air forces were linked to continual influence, notably in basing rights, training, and the provision of spares and maintenance. Thus, the Anglo-Ceylonese 1947 Defense Agreement that was part of the independence process allowed Britain to use the island's naval and air facilities in future emergencies, notably the major harbor at Trincomalee. This agreement lasted until the 1956 Suez Crisis led Ceylon (now Sri Lanka) to abrogate the agreement in a protest at British action.

In turn, concerned about the availability of harbor bases, British planners planned a new emphasis on carrier-based air power deployed in the Indian Ocean, which encouraged navalists to press for a new generation of large carriers. This was another instance of the strengthened maritime component to geopolitics presented by the air age, one that prefigured submarine-launched ballistic missiles. British interest in power projection was shown by the unrealized proposal for a naval base in Western Australia as well as an integrated Commonwealth Far East fleet.[15] To provide nuclear strike capability, US carriers had their flight decks strengthened in the early 1950s, while steam catapults for launching were used beginning in 1951. Aircraft carrying nuclear bombs required more fuel for their greater range and were therefore heavier.

In domestic geopolitical terms, the political, economic, and cultural rise of California were all important to air power. Convair, Lockheed, Douglas, and North American aircraft manufacturers were all concentrated in Los Angeles County. The large-scale components industry expanded this geoeconomic and geopolitical weight.

Yet geopolitics is precisely that, not a geographical determination of politics but a politics that reflects on geography. Thus, the response to the North Korean invasion of South Korea, and later to Chinese intervention, was far from inevitable. There had been indications in the winter of 1949–50 that the United States did not see South Korea as within its defense line, but in 1950 there was a US response that Kim Il Sung of North Korea had not anticipated. In turn, the Korean War strengthened the Western alliance and led to US support of Taiwan. Far from being a controlled limited war, this was a conflict that escalated in unexpected ways and where deterrence did not work. Chinese intervention in late 1950 was a key instance of both.

Politics, moreover, should be understood in the widest sense, as including policy formation and differences within government.[16] Thus, in the early 1950s, there was debate in the United States not so much, as in the late 1940s, about whether it should commit against Communism but, rather, how far interventionism should extend. There had been talk of the "rollback" of the Soviets in Eastern Europe. Indeed, during the 1952 elections, the Republicans, some of whom accused the Truman administrations (1945–53) of having "lost" China, had rejected "containment" as too passive, called for rollback, and spoke of "captive nations" in Eastern Europe. This was a way to present the government as having squandered the legacy of World War II.

In reality, US policy in Europe was to be much muted. US Cold War policy as a whole was defined in 1953 as a result of Project Solarium, named after the Solarium Room in the White House where Eisenhower found his Cabinet and government split on the response to Soviet expansionism and NSC 68 inadequate as a guide. As a result, alternative policy evaluations were considered, including a more nuclear posture, and containment was reaffirmed. US nuclear strength was to be built up, but

measures short of war followed.[17] The document itself
lacked attention to geographical detail but, nevertheless,
alongside the broader emphases on nuclear strength and
alliances, made reference to particular geographical areas. There were references to holding "vital areas and lines
of communication" and the protection of "a mobilization
base ... adequate to insure victory in the event of general
war."

Allies were seen as crucial:

> The effective use of U.S. strategic air power against the
> USSR will require overseas bases on foreign territory for
> some years to come. Such bases will continue indefinitely
> to be an important additional element of U.S. strategic air
> capability and to be essential to the conduct of the military
> operations on the Eurasian continent in case of general
> war. . . .
>
> Certain other countries, such as IndoChina or Formosa
> [Taiwan], are of such strategic importance to the United
> States that an attack on them probably would compel the
> United States to react with military force either locally at
> the point of attack or generally against the military power
> of the aggressor.[18]

During the Hungarian crisis of 1956, there was no
military response to the Soviet deployment of forces to
crush Hungarian independence. Instead, the discussion
of options then and earlier was instructive about how the
geopolitics of containment, if such a phrase can be used,
did not necessarily mean any particular policy. It also encompassed a number of national traditions, such as the
Christian imperialism of right-wing Portuguese geopolitics. It was also necessary to bring in change through time.
Thus, the need for military cuts in the face of financial

difficulties, as for the British navy after the two world wars and in the 1960s, does not really correspond to geopolitical arguments. Nor does the related reconceptualization of the goals and means.

The coexistence of specific strategic geopolitics with options, both over the choice between these as well as their implementation, was also the case with emphases on particular fronts of containment. The key instance was the balance in US commitments between Europe and Asia, insofar as each could be reified. This was not a fixed ratio nor indeed necessarily a matter of "holding the line" in one area such that the situation was stabilized elsewhere: as with the argument today that Taiwan is being protected in Ukraine.

Another key element of choice was provided by the atomic strategy pursued and the relevant force structure.[19] In particular, there was the question whether it would be appropriate as well as possible to use tactical nuclear weapons while preventing the cataclysm of a strategic-level, all-out nuclear war. As with other aspects of geopolitics, clarity was less obvious than assertion in this case.

The US sense of a "bomber gap" in the mid-1950s followed the identification of Soviet long-range heavy bombers beginning in 1953. This led to a new geopolitics that focused more closely on the polar routes to vulnerability and attack. In the United States, there was a stepping up of the bomber program, secret aerial reconnaissance of the Soviet Union, and the construction of extensive early-warning radar systems in Canada designed to warn of Soviet attacks over the Arctic: the Pinetree Network in 1954 and the Distant Early Warning (DEW) and

Mid-Canada Lines, both in 1957. The North American Air Defense Command, established in 1958, was important to the development of joint air-defense systems involving the US and Canada. To attack over the North Pole, the United States had constructed a base at Thule in northwest Greenland in 1951–52, a base able to stage and refuel US bombers.

The new geopolitics rested not only on weapons technology, notably the deployment beginning in 1955 of the B-52 Stratofortress with its eight Pratt and Whitney J57-P-IW turbojets, its combat range of 3,600 miles without the need to refuel, and its payload of thirty tons of bombs. The capabilities were to be enhanced from the late 1950s by aerial refueling. Constant airborne B-52 alert flights began in 1958.[20] As a reminder of the multiple military technologies involved in geopolitics, the B-52s were complemented by the four US supercarriers built in 1954–58, as some of their aircraft could carry nuclear bombs, albeit over much shorter ranges.

There was also an intellectual mastering of territory, with the possibilities that offered for a differing intensity for geopolitical knowledge. This took place at a number of levels. The SAGE (Semi-Automatic Ground Environment) Air Defense system established in 1958 reflected US investment in new technology and involved the largest computers ever built. SAGE enabled prediction of the trajectory of aircraft and missiles. The internet was to be developed and funded by the Defense Department's Defense Advanced Research Projects Agency (DARPA) to help scientists using large computers to communicate with each other.[21] At a different scale, in Western Europe, new all-weather aircraft were embedded in a NATO Air

Defense Ground Environment, an early-warning system that layered fighters, long-range nuclear missiles, and short-range tactical surface-to-air missiles.

In theoretical terms, there was a confidence that air power had transformed the situation. Air Marshal Sir John Slessor wrote in 1954: "Do not let us be distracted by geopolitical talk about heartlands, which was all very well in Mackinder's day but ceased to be relevant with the advent of the long-range bomber."[22]

Specific geopolitical factors were mentioned frequently by US commentators during the Cold War. Two obvious ones were the Domino Theory and the argument that the Soviet intervention in Afghanistan in 1979 was a threat to the Western position in the Persian Gulf.

The Domino Effect or Theory, argued that the fall of one country in Asia to Communism would lead to that of others. President Dwight Eisenhower enunciated the Domino Theory in a press conference on April 7, 1954. Eisenhower was questioned on the strategic importance of Indochina:

> First of all, you have the specific value of a locality in its production of materials that the world needs.
>
> Then you have the possibility that many human beings pass under a dictatorship that is inimical to the free world.
>
> Finally, you have broader considerations that might follow what you would call the "falling domino" principle. You have a row of dominoes set up, you knock over the first one, and what will happen to the last one is the certainty that it will go over very quickly. So you could have a beginning of a disintegration that would have the most profound influences . . . the loss of Indochina, of Burma, of Thailand, of the Peninsula [Malaya], and Indonesia following. . . . The geographical position achieved thereby does many things. It

turns the so-called island defensive chain of Japan, Formosa [Taiwan], of the Philippines to the southward; it moves in to threaten Australia and New Zealand.

It takes away, in its economic aspects, that region that Japan must have as a trading area or Japan, in turn, will have only one place in the world to go—that is, toward the Communist areas in order to live.

So, the possible consequences of the loss are just incalculable to the free world.[23]

The image of the Domino Theory, one readily taken from a game, an image that was easy to communicate to politicians and public, encouraged the US government to take a greater interest in the course and consequence of the Western retreat from empire. The Communist takeover in China was followed by effective Chinese support for the anti-French insurrection in Indochina. This led to US financial backing for the French. In turn, once the Communists had taken over in North Vietnam in 1954, the United States was concerned that a failure to support South Vietnam and to neutralize Laos would lead to the further spread of Communism in Southeast Asia.

The Domino Theory also lay behind US-backed intervention in Cuba in 1961 in the Bay of Pigs episode, as it was feared that the island would be the basis for the spread of Soviet influence in Latin America. This intervention, and its total defeat at the Bay of Pigs, was also an instance of rollback and a warning about its vulnerability, although, looked at differently, there was a failure to provide sufficient force, notably air cover, to this end. Yet again, this discussion underlined the essentially politicized nature of the discussion of geopolitics and the difficulty of applying the concepts without such politicization.

The Domino Effect was also offered in support of Western commitments in the Mediterranean and Middle East. Thus, US troops were sent to Lebanon in 1958 in response to the Eisenhower Doctrine announced in 1957 in which the United States promised aid against the spread of Communism. Already, in 1957, assistance had accordingly been provided to Jordan, although the doctrine was not formally advanced in this case. The US deployment in 1958 was instrumental to the end of the crisis.[24] The British deployment of forces to Jordan the same year was part of the same anti-Egyptian stance[25] and was followed by military support for Kuwait against Iraqi expansionist claims in 1961. These interventions were both responses to crises in particular countries and designed to prevent a sequential collapse of pro-Western governments. Thus, Kuwait was seen as the forward place for the gulf.

In practice, geopolitical linkages were complex. Thus, as a prime instance of the varied nature of outcomes, the Vietnam War indeed led to the Communist takeover of South Vietnam, Laos, and Cambodia but not of Thailand nor Malaysia. At a different level, that of priorities, in 1965–66, during the Vietnam War, the United States had supported the military overthrow of the left-leaning nationalist government of Indonesia, the setting for the non-aligned 1955 Asia-Africa Conference at Bandung, and its replacement by a pro-Western government. This provided the West with a strategic depth for Southeast Asia, and thus the geopolitical consequences of defeat in the Vietnam War were lessened greatly. The extent to which this transition could be readily conceptualized in terms of a movement or thickening of the "rimland" is more instructive about the difficulties of applying geopolitical ideas.

At the same time, the relative ease with which Indonesia—a large state, the fourth most populous in the world and one with significant natural resources, notably oil—transformed its affiliations posed a question about the idea of two coherent blocs and also an obvious interplay of heartland and rimland. Moreover, as another instance of the same, the Vietnam War was soon followed by Vietnam at war with China and its protégés in Cambodia. This war began with rivalry among the protégés, which, in turn, led to a full-scale Vietnamese invasion of Cambodia in 1978 to which China replied in 1979 by attacking Vietnam. As in the case of so many geopolitical analyses, it is possible to present this crisis in two lights. One involved China trying to prevent encirclement by the Soviet Union and its Vietnamese protégé. The other was of China also trying to anchor US support by presenting itself as a clear opponent of the Soviet Union.[26]

Indeed, the plasticity of geopolitics was fully demonstrated by the Sino-Soviet split and its consequences. This took precedence over geopolitics focused on the containment of Communism. In part, the Vietnam War provided China and the Soviet Union with the opportunity to pursue and test their rivalry, alongside weakening the United States or at least committing its forces to what was a diversion as far as China and, even more, the Soviet Union were concerned.

Such diversionary consequences proved difficult to translate to geopolitical models as the latter, notably those of containment, offered little in the form of prioritization between tasks and opportunities. Indeed, prioritization became central to the debate that surrounded the application of the models. The "debate" sounds more coherent than "debates," for, in practice, the habit of contesting priorities and ideas was far from formalized. Again, debate pushed politics to the fore. Moreover, such models said little about the psychological elements that played such a significant role in deciding where to make commitments and to what extent. An instance in the case of the Kennedy administration (1961–63) was the Catholic anti-Communism that influenced the president, notably in the cases of Cuba and Vietnam. This Catholic anti-Communism was a potent but multifaceted ideological continuum that operated in many contexts from interwar Europe to Poland in the 1980s.

As such, geopolitics was a part of the total history of the age and lacked a single trajectory. The latter was sought by the Soviet Union, which saw itself as at the revolutionary forefront but found itself unable to control the course of developments. This was latent from the outset in the tension between a unidirectional party philosophy and practice and the frictions offered by a variety of circumstances and by the moves of others.

There was a geostrategic mismatch over Vietnam. The Soviet Union provided aid to the North Vietnamese, notably surface-to-air missiles, which increased the risk and cost of using US airpower, but both were modest compared to the US commitment. Convenience played a role. The United States could intervene in Vietnam as they could not in inland Laos, which had been central to an international crisis in 1962 when the US opposed the Communist advance. Inland states could attract US intervention, as did Afghanistan beginning in 2001, but could also enjoy a measure of protection, as with the Serbian position in Kosovo in 1999. In South Vietnam, the

Americans benefited from the major cities being on or near the coast. Ports provided a transoceanic lift that air power could not. At the same time, carriers could offer air power that was closer than land bases in, for example, Guam and Thailand. This meant that it was easier to re- place fuel and weapons load more rapidly. More gener- ally, carriers offered a different geopolitics, one free of concerns about adequate airbases, overflight rights, and maintenance. Aerial refueling also extended range in a way that changed geopolitical considerations based on simple measures of range.

For political reasons, the United States could not attack the effective industrial capacity of North Vietnam, which was located in China and the Soviet Union. But the com- mitment to Vietnam was pushed to the fore to show that the US could, would, and therefore must act. As such, the US wished to demonstrate that it would not be dissuaded by the difficulties of the task, or the use of the conflict by the Communist great powers as a proxy war and diver- sionary conflict, or by domestic or international criticism as well as the search for a possible political settlement. For the US, this was a geopolitics of attitude.

One significant aspect of the situation was the US re- fusal to accept the degree to which they shared the space and the initiative with their opponents and did so in a fashion that varied across Vietnam, with physical and human geographies both playing a role, as they had also done in previous conflicts.[27] Indeed, this was a classic instance of conflict as geopolitics, with the latter under- stood as operating at a different scale to the conventional one. On a model used elsewhere, as in China, there was a determination by the Communists to employ violence to win social control, weakening opponents by the assassination of their leaders and other measures of intimidation that ensured that the government forces operated in what in theory was a vacuum. This was a geopolitics of the localities, one, common to insurgencies, in which there was a determination to force the government troops back to their bases and thus create a secure basis for the operation of the insurgents.

This sharing came to the fore with the Vietcong and North Vietnamese Tet offensive of early 1968, a surprise assault that caused major difficulties but was defeated. Again, the latter demonstrated the significance of attitudes. However misleadingly, the offensive contributed greatly—within the United States, in its alliance system, and more widely—to a sense of crisis in the US world order, a crisis that suggested that the United States was losing the Cold War and certainly the initiative. Given the significance of impressions to willpower in this case, geopolitics meant in part a field of battle, notably the contested city of Hué, that had clear political consequences.

So also, at least in design, with the US air attack on North Vietnam. Again there was a fusion of place and policy, creating a geopolitics that was turned into a strategy. US policymakers, seeking to contain the struggle, were reluctant to pursue the open targeting of an all-out, subnuclear assault. Instead, there was a belief that the measures taken beginning in 1965 could help determine North Vietnamese choices and resolve. That was not in the event the case.

The large-scale US use of aircraft represented a stand-off application of violence that contrasted with the standard aspect of insurrectionary warfare—namely, a determination to close any such gaps. This was more generally the contrast between the geostrategies involved in asymmetrical warfare.

At the same time, global geopolitics was being totally reshaped by Sino-Soviet struggles. Focusing on the Third World, Mao Zedong, the Chinese leader, claimed that the real division was between North and South, not West and East, and argued that the Soviet project was like that of the Western powers, that they both pursued imperialism. Border conflict in 1969 made the rift readily apparent and thereby altered global geopolitics for all powers. This greatly complicated the theme of civilizational, or at least essential, struggle between Communist and non-Communist blocs.

In turn, the range of Communist strategies now on offer encouraged a sense of flux, one that accentuated the possibilities for a range of non-Communist strategies, as with West German *Ostpolitik*, a reaching out for better relations with East Germany, Eastern Europe, and the Soviet Union that was intended to bring stability. Thus, the inner-German border between East and West Germany became, in West German eyes, a would-be zone for conciliation as well as confrontation. There were other elements at play, including a decreased reliance on the United States that possibly prefigures current tendencies, and notably if Donald Trump becomes president.

In addition, the factor of politics was present at the time with the SPD (Social Democratic Party) under Willy Brandt (chancellor, 1969–74), the first SPD chancellor of West Germany, seeking better relations with Eastern Europe, a process continued under his SPD successor Helmut Schmidt (chancellor, 1974–82). This was not so much a reaction against the Atlanticism of the previous Christian Democrat chancellors as a bringing to the fore of another tendency in German geopolitics but in a particular political context. The Russian question has been one for German leaders since the early eighteenth century when the buffers of the Swedish Empire and a strong Poland collapsed in the face of repeated Russian successes. *Ostpolitik* could appear as another iteration of the compromise with Russia if not, to critics, propitiation, following (very differently) Bismarck, Weimar in the 1920s, and (briefly) Hitler; but that was not how it appeared to the SPD leaders.

This situation highlighted the degree to which the period of an apparent clear-cut and clearly formed geopolitical antagonism of the 1950s was exceptional rather than the norm. This was a theme that was to be exploited by Henry Kissinger, national security adviser in 1969–75 and secretary of state in 1973–77, who sought to exploit the clashing geopolitical interests of China and the Soviet Union. As such, Kissinger underplayed the extent of ideological, political, and cultural tension within the Communist bloc: his realpolitik was another form of misleading rationalism.

The development of the range of weaponry in the age of aircraft and missiles altered the varied factors of geography. This was demonstrated in the Cuban missile crisis. Whereas in 1898, when the United States and Spain had fought over Cuba, the time constraints for intelligence gathering and transmission and for force deployment and movement were set by the technologies of the steam age, in 1962 the air age provided much more rapid moves, as in the U-2 flights over Cuba, the processing of the resulting information, and the preparations for attack. This did not, however, necessarily increase the ability to understand and, separately, control events. Indeed, effective crisis management in a speeded-up environment is both difficult and makes it harder to decide what is entailed by the geopolitical context and even conjuncture.

Contrasting national legacies, priorities, and opportunities added to the complexity. Thus, in military terms, the United States and Britain continued to place an emphasis in the 1950s on strategic bombing, one greatly enhanced by the availability of nuclear weapons. In contrast, although the Soviet Union had effective long-range bombers and an expanding navy, as it had not had during World War II, the stress there was on the army and on ground support for it from the aircraft. For all these powers, the planned application of nuclear weaponry moved from aircraft to missiles.

In China, the stress was also on land forces. There, the legacy of World War II, when air operations in China against Japan had been handled by the United States, was compounded by the revolutionary character of Maoist military thought, which also emphasized such forces and had an antitechnological dimension, even though there was also a commitment to new weaponry, certainly in the forms of jet aircraft and missiles.

Assumptions about the military context, notably in the form of specific national strategic cultures, were expressed by the spatial organizations of forces, not only their deployment but also the structural allocation of units in terms of land, sea, and air commands. These were tied to strategic tasks, and clarified geopolitical areas of concern and commitment. This was seen for example in the command structures of NATO, the Warsaw Pact, and individual states, notably the United States, as with the establishment of US Atlantic Command and Indo-Pacific Command, both in 1947, and (differently) of Central Command in 1983. Moreover, zones of concern, such as NATO's Sea Lines of Communication defense zone, and the comparable Soviet Bastion defense zone to protect the submarine concentration on the Kola Peninsula, helped shape planning and thus created a relevant geopolitics, however misleading this might be in terms of intentions in the event of conflict. Thus, the Soviets were less interested in challenging North Atlantic sea lanes than NATO believed.[28]

In addition, the spatial organizations of joint commands reflected a strong awareness of the value of joint operations, notably of air-sea cooperation and of its counterparts. In part, geopolitics in this form was therefore an aspect of force structure and a way to foster a designed outcome. This was an instance of geopolitics as organizational context and, to a degree, content.

The realpolitik of détente in the early and mid-1970s was replaced in the late 1970s by a growing US return under President Jimmy Carter (1977–81) to confrontation. The Iranian and Afghan crises provided a geopolitical context to this shift. However, there was also a rejection by Carter of the Soviet system, one based on his opposition to the Soviet stance on human rights.[29]

The Cold War came to a renewed apex of tension in the early 1980s, with nuclear war apparently a prospect in 1983. There were more specific conflicts in Afghanistan, Central America, Angola, and the Middle East. In each case, the major power had only limited control over its protégés, but there was a sense that for the United States or the Soviet Union to permit failure on the part of its protégés would be to endanger credibility and therefore the entire system. In this respect, there was not so much the geopolitics of specific zones and particular concerns but rather a geopolitics in which everything was involved and, once made, commitments were difficult to reverse.

The Soviet invasion of Afghanistan in December 1979 was a classic instance of the difficulties with simplistic geopolitical modeling of the "geography is destiny" type. It also provided an example of the limited value in moving in commentary from the conjunctural to the historical, for the latter was frequently deployed as a context, with extensive reference to the "Great Game" of Anglo-Russian competition in the nineteenth century and on into the twentieth. In practice, a number of factors played a role in an intervention that had really begun not as a consequence of a Soviet master plan but as a result of short-term tensions in Afghan politics coming to a bloody inconstancy. In 1973, Zahir Shah, the monarch, was overthrown by his cousin and brother-in-law Mohammed Daoud Khan, a former prime minister. Backed by a group of Soviet-trained officers, this was a coup for modernization, as also with the overthrow of monarchy in Egypt (1952) and Iraq (1958). Khan was willing to accommodate the Soviet Union, and the coup was seen as an extension of Soviet influence. It increased, but he was a nationalist, not a Communist.

In turn, in the Saur Revolution in 1978, Daoud was overthrown and killed in a coup mounted by the Soviet-backed People's Democratic Party of Afghanistan. The misnomer nature of the party was rapidly displayed in

the rebellions provoked by its unpopular forced modernization. These rebellions were met with brutality by the
divided government, which itself had a coup from within
in September 1979. This was unwelcome to the Soviet
government.

How that situation accorded with geopolitical modeling was unclear, and indeed Afghanistan received scant
attention from the international commentariat. It was
an unstable client state but one of limited consequence
compared to Iran, where the pro-Western shah had been
overthrown in January 1979. Indeed, it was the latter that
focused US regional concern, not least with greater anxiety about the Persian Gulf.

Indeed, this anxiety captured the extent to which Cold
War geopolitics were far less focused and consistent than
might be suggested by a phrase of that type. The Americans devoted much of their attention not to the Soviet
Union but to a string of lesser powers. Some, notably
China, North Korea, North Vietnam, and Cuba, could
be fitted into the model by reference to Soviet influence.
However, this model and Communist ideology were of
no value to understanding Iran and were of scant use with
Iraq, a Soviet ally but very much driven by its dictator, including in an opposition to Iran that led to a major war in
1980–88, an opposition that suited US interests. Concern
about the Iranian Revolution helped provide the United
States with a motive that drew also on economic interest in the shape of oil supplies, but the establishment of
US Central Command as an organizing body for the US
military commitment in the region, in turn, encouraged
a hostile US response to a range of developments that
would probably have better been approached indirectly.[30]

Meanwhile, encouraging concern with Middle Eastern developments, the oil crisis of 1979 contributed to a global economic downturn that helped the United States into recession in 1980. More specifically as a mood setter, the humiliation of the failure to rescue the US hostages held captive by Iranian radicals in the US embassy in Tehran, especially the unsuccessful rescue mission of April 1980, produced a sense of failure, with geopolitics shrinking to the significance of an inherently minor episode, prefiguring the later response to American losses (eighteen killed) in the Black Hawk Incident in Mogadishu, Somalia, in 1993. The deadly Islamic terrorist attacks on New York and Washington in 2001 were far more major incidents but again captured a shrinking of geopolitics in that the far-ranging response of the war on terror was triggered by a highly specific incident.

The more general international situation had changed as a result of the responses to the Soviet military intervention in Afghanistan in December 1979 in which the government was violently overthrown and a protégé installed. This provided the direct Cold War action conspicuously lacking in Iran, where the theocratic revolutionaries kept the Soviet Union at a distance. Indeed, the Ayatollah Khomeini, the leader of the Islamic Revolution and the Guardian of the Islamic Republic, described the Soviet Union as "the other Great Satan." Furthermore, when, two days after the Soviet invasion of Afghanistan, the Soviet envoy in Iran promised Khomeini assistance in any conflict with the United States, he was told that there could be no mutual understanding between a Muslim nation and a non-Muslim government. This was a very different—that is, religious—geopolitics to that which was conventionally understood, but such a geopolitics was of great longevity.

As an instance of the number of elements involved, the Soviet intervention in Afghanistan arose from many factors. A key one was that of an unstable borderland, the factor that had also led to the invasions of Hungary (1956) and Czechoslovakia (1968). There was an unwillingness to see a client state collapse and a fear that problems could spill over into Soviet Tajikistan. More generally, Central Asia had a religious and cultural identity that Russian rule and Sovietization had lessened but not ended. There was also anxiety that the Afghan government might turn to China, thus extending the threat to Soviet borderlands.

In terms of a Soviet "advance," there was the military dimension of closer air proximity to the Persian Gulf and the ability to put pressure on neighboring Pakistan, an ally of China and an enemy of India, a key Soviet ally.

As so often with geopolitics, it was not so much the action, both intention and implementation, that was the key element but, instead, the response, again both attitude and action. Western alarmism was accompanied by pressure for action, both there and elsewhere. In his State of the Union address to Congress in January 1980, President Jimmy Carter warned that the Afghan invasion "could pose the most serious threat to peace since the Second World War," which was an exaggeration that testified to the alarmism of the period and that looked toward the exaggeration of the country's significance by US policymakers in the early twenty-first century. The Soviet invasion was treated not as a frontier policing operation designed to ensure a pliant government but as an act of aggression that had to be countered for containment to work. This view drew on a tendency, seen throughout the Cold War, to exaggerate Soviet political ambitions and military capability. In part, this reflected the degree to which there is very little politically that can be gained from arguing that threats are being exaggerated. Instead, it is the opposite that is the case.

There is no simple divide here between "the military" and "politicians." Instead, both can be reified in a misleading fashion and one, moreover, that ignores the degree to which military leaders are also politicians. As such, the extent to which they were able to present their views was significant and varied, both by state and also with time. Institutional and political changes, for example, in Britain the loss of the separate service ministries in 1964, were highly relevant in this process.[31] In part, geopolitical arguments were an aspect of the process of lobbying or politicking by defense politicians.

However, pushing geopolitical conceptions to the fore and comparably encouraging the idea of strategic culture, it was difficult for the United States to acquire accurate information about the Soviet Union, whether over Afghanistan or more generally. The Soviet Union was a closed society with a determination to keep policy differences as well as its capabilities secret. So also with China.

However, this acute tension was to be reversed as relations improved between the United States and the Soviet Union in the late 1980s, with Soviet forces withdrawing from Afghanistan and, as part of the end of the Cold War, a marked reduction in differences over Angola and Central America. These became both preludes and accompaniments to an unraveling that extended, in an unintended fashion, to the end of the Communist position in Eastern

Europe in 1989 and, then, in 1991, to the fall of the Soviet
Union. To Vladimir Putin, in his state-of-the-nation address in 2005, this "was the greatest geopolitical catastrophe
of the century," had left many millions of Russians living
in foreign countries (an argument employed by German
revanchists in the 1920s and 1930s), and had fostered separatist movements within Russia. As with many statements
employing geopolitics, there was no real suggestion of any
precise usage. Although geopolitical thinkers saw themselves as influential, geopolitics as practical is rather about
assumptions and actions than the application of theory.
The idea of geopolitical defeat, however, was an important
one, and it helped explain the link for Russia from the Cold
War to a humiliating and dangerous postwar situation that
had to be remedied. Thus, geopolitics became a term meaning "should be," as is more generally the case with concepts.
The difference is provided by the degree to which commentators accept this point, one shared, for example, with the
related concept of strategic culture.

The geopolitics of the 1980s had a strong geofinancial
character. The marked expansion of capital availability
in the world made it possible to cover the ever-widening
federal deficit in the United States, one that owed much to
a failure to increase taxation in order to fund expenditure.
This had been the case with the Vietnam War and was
also so with the Reaganite arms buildup in the 1980s. The
reinvestment of oil revenues in the United States ensured
that petrodollars became a measure of US influence and,
in turn, meant that it was necessary for the United States
to maintain its position in the Middle East.

Similarly, the beneficiaries of East Asian economic
growth, particularly Japan, which had become the world's

second largest economy, invested in the United States, thus helping the Americans to finance imports from East Asia and, in particular, to draw on both the economic growth of Japan and the strategic asset of Chinese cooperation. Moreover, under the US umbrella, there were no serious issues in dispute between China and Japan. The Soviet refusal to make any concession over returning to Japan the Kurile Islands, seized in 1945, ensured that the Soviets passed up the possibility of massive Japanese investment in the Soviet Far East, which therefore remained undeveloped and unable to threaten China or to offset the US-Chinese rapprochement.

The geopolitical alignment with capital-rich East Asia and the Middle East was encouraged by the ending in 1984 by the Reagan government of the withholding tax on interest on income paid to nonresidents. This encouraged the large-scale foreign purchase of Treasury bonds, which helped contain inflation and finance rising military expenditure. Moreover, attractive US interest rates in the 1980s kept the demand strong and ensured that global capital flows focused on the United States, which put heavy pressures on the states that had borrowed heavily in the 1970s, notably in Eastern Europe but also in South America. In a sense, the 1980s helped bring further to fruition US hopes in the mid-1940s that economic liberalism would spread US influence.

Indeed, the United States' vulnerability to domestic discontent or division over the geopolitical confrontations of the Cold War were assuaged by the ability to fund its commitments. This ability had hit a crisis in the early 1970s with the heavy burden of Vietnam added to other Cold War commitments, notably in Europe, South

Korea, and the Mediterranean, and these impacting an economy affected by declining effectiveness vis-à-vis the rising competitiveness of West Germany and Japan in a context of fixed exchange rates and then the shock of the oil price hike. There had been a slow postcrisis economic and financial restrengthening, before the fresh public financial pressures of Reaganomics, but the potential flaws of the latter in geoeconomic terms were lessened by the widespread stakes, domestic and international, in the system. The collapse of the Soviet bloc in 1989–91 helped ensure that the much-discussed US policy drawbacks of the 1980s did not culminate in failure.

—∿∿—

SIX

AN ASCENDANT
WORLD ORDER SLIPS
UNDER PRESSURE,
1989–2021

THE PRESENT EVER SLIPS INTO the past, and so with analysis that attempts to shape both, not least as part of a quest to engage with the future. The period from the end of the Cold War to the early 2020s saw a switchback of patterning and predictions as different themes and crises came to the fore. Western perspectives tend to dominate in this matter. Indeed, one of the major problems with the literature of and about geopolitics is that these perspectives are to the fore. Yet there was also a switchback in other countries as the contents and contexts of politics, domestic and international, changed greatly or were transformed. This was seen, for example, in China, notably in response to domestic politics and to the example elsewhere of advanced US military technology.[1]

And so also with geopolitical discussion: as so often, especially when considering the United States, military factors were prominent, although the strength of the US economy and its central place in the global economic and fiscal systems underpinned this situation. Looked at differently (and the contrast is instructive), there was not so much an underpinning as a separation between these two forms of dominance: they were clearly linked by many commentators, but the impact was more varied at the level of responses to US power.

The period began with geopolitical attention focused on Eastern Europe and the collapse of Communist and Soviet control in Eastern Europe without war. By the end of 1991, this had spread to the Soviet Union itself, but there was no comparable change in China. Moreover, attention was refocused in 1991 on a war in Kuwait in which a US-led coalition defeated Iraqi invaders. This began a period of direct US intervention different from the earlier sponsorship of Israel and arm's-length role in the 1980–88 Iran-Iraq War.

In one respect, 1991 was another Middle Eastern war, but the 1990s saw a range of conflicts in a broader area, including the Caucasus and the Bosnia and Kosovo crises. To a degree, older fault lines, some religious or ethnic, emerged to affect regional geopolitics.

The European Union sought to play a role in the geopolitics of Eastern Europe, the Balkans, and the Mediterranean, seeking to offer stabilization, but this proved more successful in the northern part of Eastern Europe than in a Balkans made unstable by the fragmentation of Yugoslavia. Meanwhile, in the Muslim world, pan-Islamism played a role as did an authoritarianism that was to suppress liberalism and Islamism from Iraq in 1991 to Syria, Algeria, and Egypt in the 2010s.

The 1990s and early 2000s appeared to offer a hyperpower, the United States, able to use transformative military technology to reach everywhere in an apogee of air-mindedness. That was very much a theme of the "revolution in military affairs" (RMA), a paradigm shift in capability trumpeted by US commentators, before being succeeded by the concept of transformation, one in which the United States was in the lead. Air power now had a direct satellite component, with real-time reconnaissance closing the gap between sensors and firers. This was seen as having major consequences in the defeat of Iraqi field forces in 2003, and that was a major leap forward in capability from the rapid success seen over the Iraqis in 1991. Guided bombs were a key component of battlefield accuracy and helped ensure that the three-dimensional battlefield could be dominated by air power.

Mass had its own weight, but mass in 1991 was increasingly seen not in the number of troops. In part, this was because of the type of struggle involved: troops numbers are more significant for counterinsurgency struggles as was to be demonstrated in Iraq after its conquest in 2003. The United States then suffered seriously from a shortage of troops that was borne of inadequate prewar planning for the aftermath of conflict. It was as if US planners, notably the secretary of defense, Donald Rumsfeld, believed the propaganda about the RMA, although, in addition, they made the classic mistake of propounding attitudes and devising plans that were appropriate for the military that was readily available: in 2003, the US-led coalition was far smaller than in 1991, while the United States had fewer forces to deploy.

Aside from justified complaints about systemic hubris, much of the criticism of US war making in recent decades has been one focused on the failure to clarify the goals of conflict and thus the political as well as military objectives.[2] That is a plausible criticism but also inadequate because a lack of clarity is often understandable as is the determination to limit the military commitment, a related cause of criticism from commentators, both civilian and in the armed forces. The lack of clarity in part reflects the changeable nature both of circumstances in the zone of conflict and more generally. Moreover, this changeable nature can have highly significant consequences as with the consequences of the Sino-Soviet split for US options in the Vietnam War. The absence of a similar division ensured that the Korean War posed a very different strategic challenge, as, today, does the Ukraine conflict.

Strategic clarity, separately, can be a way to signal to opponents, allies, and supporters that a state may not persist or that it has boxed in its options. As such, it lessens, even throws away, political possibilities, including compromise and abandonment, or burdens them with a high political and reputational cost. Commentators, especially US ones, can juxtapose post-1945 conflict with World War II, but that is to overlook the extent to which the US experience in 1941–45 was untypical in that other powers could fight a "limited war" of a sort, for example, the Soviet Union not fighting Japan until August 1945. Moreover, if the period 1939–45 or 1937–45 is considered, then the United States took part in an important but limited struggle with the Axis powers until December 1941.

The problems posed by the failure to triumph in Afghanistan and Iraq led to a revival of more established themes. However, the emphasis was not on the great power competition that, instead, was to come to the fore beginning in the late 2010s. Rather, there was a stress on borderlands and the difficulties of controlling them. This emphasis was also projected into the past, notably in

Alfred Rieber's *The Struggle for the Eurasian Borderlands: From the Rise of Early Modern Empires to the End of the First World War* (2014), with its theme that the situations in the borderlands of empires are crucial to the stability of the latter, with patterns of conflict determined by complex, interconnected, and fluid frontiers. This approach underplayed the key corresponding feature that choice was involved in where the frontiers were sought and borderlands thus created. For example, in the 1960s, US policymakers envisaged South Vietnam as a frontier, only to find that their inability to create that borderland or, rather, sustain their image of it as a frontier led to defeat.

Apparent US control in the 1990s was expressed through confidence in economic predominance, fiscal weight, and a military system of global potency. There was scant sense in this that geographical factors should act as a constraint. Indeed, the US mantra of "enlargement and engagement" was at once highly geopolitical and anti- or a-geopolitical in its complete ignorance and disregard of local, regional, and even global realities. US restraint, as in withdrawing from Somalia in 1994, was a response to risk, unclear purpose, and a reluctance to accept low casualties rather than an awareness that forces could not be deployed. US power was to be punctuated by enforced withdrawals, Saigon in 1975 being the key instance, whereas Afghanistan in 2021 was a withdrawal of choice.

At the same time, these withdrawals themselves were products of US power, such that it could be widely projected around the world. Moreover, perception was a key element, notably in whether the emphasis should be on projection or withdrawal. There was also the question of effectiveness. Thus, US forces were to return to Somalia beginning in 2007 in targeting Al-Shabaab by airstrikes and the use of special forces. Furthermore, as China became more hostile to the United States in the early twenty-first century, so Vietnam, in opposition, became more friendly.

Returning to the 1990s, reliance on air power alone in the Bosnia and Kosovo crises of 1995 and 1999 raised instructive questions about effectiveness, power projection, and the extent to which air power could serve to energize or support more local forces. As a result, geopolitics operated at a number of levels.

There was bitter debate within the United States over US peacekeeping missions and whether this weakened the military as well as leading the US into unwelcome commitments. In part, there was shared worry within the military about being drawn in essentially to solve political issues, and that at a time when the size of the army was falling.[3] In part, this debate overlapped with that from the 1990s within the army between advocates of a focus on low-intensity conflicts and others who emphasized the maintenance of a focus on a restructuring for high-intensity conflicts.[4] There was a clear political aspect as well in the hostility to peacekeeping. In large part, this was a hostile reaction to the liberal internationalism of the Clinton presidencies (1993–2001), which were seen as far more interventionist than that of George H. W. Bush (1989–93), although the latter had fought Iraq in 1991.

Meanwhile, there was from the 1990s a degree of marked overconfidence about the consequences of intervention and a dangerous mixture of reacting to real or apparent dangers through trying to gain the initiative by using force. Deployment, however, while operationally often successful, did not have the necessary strategic purpose or conclusion. This was a long-standing problem but had been minimized for the United States during the late 1970s and 1980s by Cold War restraints and post-Vietnam domestic restrictions. Now, there was a different situation.

Indeed, the idea that "rogue states" and "failed states" posed a fundamental challenge to stability was one that sought to reprise the prospectus of long-range concern also enunciated by US commentators. What such states entailed was in part a matter of perception, with these views not necessarily accepted more generally as analysis or guide, including by US allies.

Yet whereas Russia, fighting for limited goals, won eventual success in Chechnya, Georgia, and Crimea, US strength, influence, and goal all, in turn, encountered serious checks, and this invited discussion about US strength and goals. This proved particularly the case with the interventions in Afghanistan and Iraq. They were designed to create the military basis for the installation of allied local politicians as the head of national governments. However, the United States found that this process involved a political wish fulfillment that could not match the strength of local opposition. Whereas in the Vietnam War the latter had had a considerable international resource, in the shape of Soviet and Chinese backing, this was not the case in Afghanistan or Iraq, but, in each, the new governments were particularly fragile. Moreover, the United States failed to appreciate the nature of local society and, insofar as they did, wanted a change in cultural norms that aroused even more opposition.[5]

Furthermore, the only partial diffusion within society of the economic benefits of globalism helped in the buildup of isolationist sentiment, notably as seen with the victory of Donald Trump in the presidential election of 2016 but also seen with the support for H. Ross Perot in the 1992 and 1996 elections. In part, this buildup was a longer-term process as the development and anchoring of the United States' alliance system from 1945, not least under the pressure of Communist expansion, entailed an internationalism, notably in investment and tariff reductions, that allowed the developing economies of Japan and West Germany to benefit greatly from US markets. This was explicitly intended to limit any chances for revanchist tendencies. While this process served geoeconomic goals in restraining costs and spreading a profitability that expanded the market for US products, it also hit hard at the job opportunities for US workers. Indeed, as every country is itself a coalition, however its government and politics are conceptualized, the US coalition was put under pressures, although as nothing compared with what was to come from the 1990s. Such coalitions were an important aspect of politics but did not necessarily have a geographical dimension.

There was also a strain on US alliance systems, a strain that was greater from the 1990s to that of earlier tensions.[6] The "cement," never strong, of a common concern about the Soviet Union was dissipated as there was no sense in the 1990s that there might be a Russian revanchism. Indeed, the defeats meted out to Iraq and its Soviet-equipped military in 1991 and 2003 indicated that former Soviet protégés could not or would not be protected by Russia, as did the overawing of Serbia in 1995 and 1999. So also with the economic weakening of the long-standing Soviet relationship with Cuba. The containment of hostile powers, such as Iran, and states judged hostile in the 1990s and 2000s was far easier for US pressure due to the absence of any Cold War dualism to offset the United States. Yet that did not mean that it was possible to dictate to these powers, as Iran and Iraq both demonstrated, and this mismatch between US intentions and outcomes encouraged the desire for action on the part of US policymakers.[7] This contributed to the strain in the United States' alliance system, one that led under President George W. Bush to the idea of the "coalition of the willing." In practice, that was scarcely new, as had been clearly seen at the time of the Vietnam War. Support then for US intervention had a certain geopolitical logic, with allied states from South Korea to Australia reflecting their concern about Communist expansionism, notably China.

In 2003, in contrast, there was no such geopolitical logic but, instead, participation in the war by an ad hoc group. Moreover, opposition from within NATO to US policy over Iraq was matched by that to NATO expansion to include Georgia and Ukraine.

These and other differences were to continue in the response to the crises over Ukraine that began in 2014. This division raised questions, in both the United States and Europe, over the viability of NATO and over the practicality of an EU foreign and defense policy. In 2022–24, hostility to the Russian invasion of Ukraine overcame these differences to an extent, but they remained strong.

Returning to the 1990s, at this point China was not able nor interested in pursuing the takeover of Russia's alliance system nor in developing a global geopolitics of independently operating states within a multipolar world. As a result, the United States was able to act as the world's leading power at a modest cost in the 1990s. It had won the Cold War in the same way in part as a result of the diversion of Soviet strength borne by China. US commentators were apt to underplay this point.

In contrast, this successful outcome and this modest cost were lost beginning in the 2000s in a major shift in the international situation that had a geopolitical component in Russo-Chinese alignment in Eurasia. That led to discussion of a loss or failure of strategy, meaning of Anglo-American strategy. However, the contingent, not to say fortuitous, character of the easier situation in the 1970s, 1980s, and 1990s did not attract sufficient attention. Already in the United States there was a sense of concern about China. Before the war on terror launched by the US in 2001, there was talk of what in effect was a "pivot to Asia," for example, in the writings and speeches of Paul Wolfowitz and Donald Rumsfeld.

Moreover, there were other developments that had particular geopolitical connotations. The use of no-fly zones, as over parts of Iraq and the former Yugoslavia, represented a particular regional geopolitics that had wider strategic consequences. So also with the continuance of base-acquisition and development policies, a process taken further by new entrants, notably China. The likely naval bases of the latter attracted particular attention, both in the Indian Ocean, especially Djibouti, where one has been established, and Gwadar (in Pakistan), and in the Pacific. On the Gulf of Thailand, China developed the Ream Naval Base in Cambodia beginning in late 2022, with a pier facility that could berth an aircraft carrier from which the Malacca Strait could be threatened.

At the same time, there are also signs of possible Chinese base projection farther afield, particularly in the Arctic and, more concretely, the Atlantic, with Cuba and Equatorial Guinea prime candidates for the latter. The frontier confrontation between India and Pakistan in 1998–99, one accompanied by India and Pakistan showing nuclear strength, was one of many that makes it difficult to think in terms of "heartland" or "rimland." India had the support of Russia and the US, and Pakistan of China and Arab states. In part, with Russia and China, this was a matter of differences going back for over three decades, but other differences and powers were fed into this. In turn, conjunctures could challenge links, as with US suspicion of Pakistan over support for terrorism in Afghanistan and elsewhere.[8]

In the case of the United States, there remained the issues over the use of Japanese bases and the need to respond to changes of policy in the Philippines, as well as to developments in relations with Panama. Britain and France took forward the idea of overseas bases, particularly in the Persian Gulf, while states that had overseas forces and therefore bases, however ad hoc, included Turkey and the United Arab Emirates.

Russia lost nearby bases as a result of the collapse of the Soviet Union, for example, air and sea bases in Estonia from which the eastern Baltic could be influenced. Russia sought, however, to retain a more distant network of bases, notably in the Caribbean thanks to Cuba and Venezuela. The Syrian crisis of the 2010s was also significant as it involved the Russian protection of its Mediterranean bases. Indeed, that is a reminder of the range of factors involved in geopolitics and of the extent to which the salience of one does not mean that it is the most significant for all the participants involved. Syria provided Russia with both naval and air bases. The value of the last at Khmeimim was enhanced by the greater range of Russian aircraft and air-launched missiles. Thus, the Tu-22 M3 version of the Backfire bomber deployed in 2019 has a range of 1,850 miles, while the cruise missiles it launches have a range of over 3,000 miles.

As a result, Russia enjoyed a projection capability that gave its bases a very different potential presence. So also with that at Kaliningrad from which the Baltic is exposed. Power projection offers a geopolitics of threat, deterrence, and denial. From this perspective, the Russian retention of Sevastopol in Crimea is a continued threat in the Black Sea, where Romania, Bulgaria, and Turkey are in NATO, and Georgia has been heavily intimidated by Russia. A naval base also offers the advantages of a protected site in which aircraft and ships can be supplied as well as protected from hostile missiles and aircraft, although, in turn, there is a concentrated target.

For China, there was the growth of rail geopolitics, the rapid development of a major fleet, and growing interest in the Pacific, the Indian Ocean, and the Arctic. Thus, in the early 2020s, China pursued attempts to develop influence in the southwest Pacific, including in the Solomon Islands, Vanuatu, Tonga, and Papua New Guinea. Visiting Vanuatu on July 27, 2003, President Macron of France warned about Chinese imperialism. He also told New Caledonia that if it broke from French rule there could be a "Chinese naval base tomorrow."

In the Indian Ocean, there were successes in winning influence in Sri Lanka, Pakistan, and Myanmar. As with the southwest Pacific, however, this is a situation in which there are considerable variations in activity and outcome alongside what is presented as a zone of activity. The respective degree of emphasis in any account reflects assumptions about subordination to a system.

The form of influence varies. Thus, the largest state-driven rail plans for the present and into the future are those of China. This is somewhat ironic as China's overseas economy is more dependent on maritime links, while the share of domestic freight moved by rail has fallen considerably over the last decade. This is an aspect of China's rising need for oil and its more long-term shift from a coal to a coal-oil economy. There are global implications for the respective use of coal and oil in terms of the ratio of imports to Chinese production and the source of these imports. Thus, coal is part of the troubled Chinese-Australian partnership.

Nevertheless, Chinese geopolitical attention also centered on the attempt to develop rail links into the Asian interior and beyond. This represented a particular type of geopolitical speculation and the focus on routes rather than the nodes of harbors and related loading and unloading facilities. There is a rail equivalent, which includes the stress on junctions and the related marshaling facilities, but the latter have never attracted the attention devoted to railway lines.

The Chinese railway boom has much to do with high-speed lines to carry passengers, troops, and, to a limited extent, high-value, low-bulk goods. The boom is driven by politics as much as economics, as in the building of a line to Lhasa in Tibet, which is seen as a way to cement control over the latter. So also with the extension of the line to near the Indian frontier, which ensured that the Chinese were able to bring up reinforcements more rapidly than India during the 2022 border crisis. As with that between China and India in 1962, this clash registered China's greater strength and thus was of geopolitical consequence in what was a pulse point between the "heartland" and the "rimland." In this specific case, the former power was stronger, although there was no inherent reason why that should have been the case. There was also a use of rail by China to extend power in Xinjiang.

Alongside the use of rail to increase power domestically, there was an international geopolitical dimension. President Xi Jinping's "Belt-and-Road" initiative adopted in 2013 saw the provision of international aid linked to the development of "rail corridors" furthering Chinese strategic interests that were at once geopolitical and economic. Thus, one was planned through Pakistan to the Indian Ocean port of Gwadar as part of the China-Pakistan Economic Corridor, although, as yet, it has not been built. In contrast the shorter railway to Vientiane, the capital of Laos, was opened in 2021 and is seen as a stage in a route to Singapore, which is regarded as part of the Trans-Asian railway network outlined in 2006. In practice, however, this network shows few signs of coming to fruition and has been affected by major tensions over cost sharing.

Meanwhile, the route of Chinese links westward through Central Asia is a matter of pressure, diplomacy, and investment. In November 2022, Mongolia opened a new rail link to China, between Zuunbayan and Khangi, to move products from mines, including Rio Tinto's Ofu Tolgoi project, to industrial hubs such as Baotou in the Chinese region of Inner Mongolia. This is one of three new rail links from Mongolia to China that were intended to boost Mongolian export capacity. Rail was presented as less expensive and quicker than the use of trucks, while the latter had been interrupted frequently due to Chinese concerns that drivers would transmit the COVID virus.

In 2022, China also signed an agreement with Kyrgyzstan and Uzbekistan that fixed the route of a proposed new railway to European markets without going through Russia as did existing links, which involved expensive changes of gauge, entailing lifting heavy wagons and placing them on new wheel assemblies. Sadyr Japarov, the president of Kyrgyzstan, emphasized this agreement as an assertion of independence from Russia. For landlocked states, such as Uzbekistan and Kyrgyzstan, rail links, respectively to China and across Afghanistan to Pakistan, offer economic and political possibilities, but there are serious political, security, and financial issues facing such plans. Earlier, to the southwest in 2016, Nepal and China agreed on a high-speed railway from Kathmandu to the Chinese border, part of the Chinese plan to win over Nepal from India. Nepal, however, cannot afford its share of the cost, which will be high due to very mountainous terrain.

Railway geopolitics has attracted much attention of late, in some respect in a reprise of themes from the late nineteenth and early twentieth centuries. However, speculation from the 2010s about developing trade from East Asia overland by rail to Western Europe was not really brought to fruition at any scale. To that extent, Mackinder's 1904 analysis proved flawed, as should have been more apparent at the time given the mismatch between rail plans and completion. The ambitious railway construction plans of China notwithstanding, there is no sign that this will change. The bulk movement of freight remains far easier by ship than by rail, in terms of bulk transport, haulage costs, and political maintenance issues.

There is also the potential for political disorder to affect rail infrastructure and options, as with the Ukraine war that began in 2022. This ended route plans via Ukraine and, more significantly for China, those across southern Russia. Yet any option for an east-west rail line farther south, although pushed by Pakistan, Iran, and Turkey, was affected by wider regional instability and the potential for more. This was notably with disaffection and instability in the Kurdish areas of Iran, Iraq, and Turkey. Although unrelated to the east-west rail link, disputes within the Caucasus also affected transport possibilities, particularly between Armenia and Azerbaijan, as well as involving separatist regions of Georgia.

As a reminder of the varied pressures that combine on geopolitics, overland trade from China to Europe has not prospered primarily for economic reasons. Railway transport costs remain stubbornly higher than shipping; indeed, as a reminder of technological and organizational factors, the switch to containers have greatly widened the gap. Rather than extrapolating recent and current trends, a tendency that is all too easy, the financial problems facing the Belt-and-Road plans indeed led to a decline in enthusiasm in the early 2020s, not least as Chinese growth rates fell. Chinese railways, old and new, help to link to a network that can move goods to Europe, but the discussion of new maritime links as a result of the melting of Arctic ice highlight the relative weaknesses of this rail network. In 2022, in contrast, the port of Hamburg and its Chinese state-owned partner COSCO, which owns the major Greek port of Piraeus and shares of those at

Antwerp, Bilbao, Hamburg, and Zeebrugge, looked at setting up joint shipping projects in Europe.

The climate change that makes polar links possible may challenge the relative economic appeal of rail, including in North America and in North Asia, while also more specifically affecting individual rail routes, not least due to permafrost melting. This last is a particular issue for rail routes across Siberia, such that it is doubtful that the Russians will build again, as they did in the 1970s and 1980s, a rail line across northern Siberia. Container travel by sea and rail faces similar issues in terms of local factors and transshipment requirements, but rail has the additional issue of being a fixed route with associated costs, as well as vulnerabilities to attack as with Ukrainian sabotage of Russian rail links in Siberia in late 2023.

The ship, in contrast, offers a possibility for adaptability that can reduce the risk dimension of the choice for sea over rail. It is instructive that sea transport is most vulnerable to attack at narrow transits, such as the Panama and Suez Canals and the Strait of Malacca. This vulnerability provides opportunities for asymmetrical conflict, including forms of maritime terrorism, as with Houthi attacks on shipping in the Bab al-Mandeb choke point at the southern end of the Red Sea in early 2024.

Despite the emphasis on rail links, and qualifying their possible development, China very much depends on maritime ones. Its energy and food imports largely come by sea, including more than half of its oil imports and half of its gas. China has 55 percent of its energy usage provided by coal, which has major implications for the geopolitics of pollution production. Yet, although it is a major coal producer, China has the largest coal imports in the world, most from Indonesia and Australia. Australia, moreover, provides 60 percent of China's iron ore requirement. China also has one of the lowest amounts of per capita arable land. This will be accentuated by desertification and affected by pressures over water availability. Indeed, in China, as in India, there are clear tensions between economic growth and the environmental problems that are posed. In one respect, these can be addressed by using the greater wealth produced by such growth to address the problems. However, there are few signs of such a benign cycle.

In addition to the international level, geopolitics at the subnational one reflected to a great extent the imprint on earlier alignments that had largely begun after World War II. Economic developments had major social consequences, with the mechanization of agriculture encouraging the movement of large numbers from the land to the cities. These became the central sites for a substantial growth in population that brought volatility and challenged preexisting patterns of deference and hierarchy, as well as more "natural" processes of life in the sense of those of rural existence. This change was the fundamental geopolitical one but did not play through the classic geopolitical agenda focused on international political rivalries. This was not least because the attempt by Communist powers to exploit social discontent had only limited political traction in terms of changing political and territorial control.

The social changes outlined above caused more pressure as a result of the major rise in the global population, which had resource implications in terms of the need for more food, water, housing, and employment. These issues often comprised a major part of national geopolitics or exacerbated the latter. To a degree, and particularly so at the international level, these might appear to be a matter of national units, but alongside this, there was much distinction, tension, and even competition between groups at the subnational level. These groups could have a geographical emphasis, even basis, as in "there were more poor in the North."

Geopolitics therefore was and is inherently fissiparous as a topic. Indeed, this range and diversity can be expanded by noting the geopolitics of particular localities. The successful, prosperous, or well-connected will tend to live in particular parts of cities, and spatial differentiation extends to retail, education, leisure, transport, social links, communication, and much else.[9] Digital analysis of activity and circumstances provides much evidence of geographical variations.

Again, some of this differentiation can be readily translated onto the international scale, as has been done by exponents of what is termed *critical geopolitics*. This has been most notably the case in a sustained hostile discussion of the spatial structures of capitalism as a system of exploitation. This critique, however, rested in part on a somewhat naive account of capitalism, not least one that generally failed to devote adequate attention to rivalry between capitalist concerns, a rivalry that could be more significant to at least these concerns than the exploitation already referred to. The relationship between critical geopolitics and developments in international relations at the state level was generally indirect, however much the language of the Global South encouraged the idea of a shared victimhood. In part, this was an account of geopolitics from the perspective of a Left that focused on such victimhood. The latter jumped national boundaries by finding oppression that was both international and domestic. Moreover, as another aspect of internationalism, the cooperation, if any, by workers with this alleged oppression was presented as a form of false consciousness by these workers.

Geopolitics after the Cold War appeared to some to be easy to explain, while others felt it lacked clear shape. The latter was linked in the 1990s to the thesis of Francis Fukuyama, advanced in particular in *The End of History and the Last Man* (1992). This thesis presented the ascendancy of Western liberal democracy as an "end-point of history" in the shape of an US-centered international order committed to this liberal democracy. As such, the latter provided a context within which those found wanting could be seen as "rogue states." This visualization of a global order left scant room for spatial division of any form or other than in terms of progress and its rejection.

The intellectual US politician Daniel Patrick Moynihan, in *Pandaemonium: Ethnicity in International Politics* (1993), emphasized territorial nationalism based on an ethnic consciousness that is not a by-product of redundant drives and got the geopolitics of the time more accurately than Fukuyama. Moynihan, however, confused ethnicity and nationalism, not least as the former could be divided, for example, by religion, and the latter could be multiethnic. An emphasis on religion was offered by Samuel P. Huntington, again a US political scientist, particularly in his *The Clash of Civilizations and the Remaking of World Order* (1996). In this, Huntington developed arguments he had made in 1992 and 1993 in which he proposed that cultural and religious identities and concerns would provide the basis for geopolitical rivalry. This was one that extended across time and space, both within and between states.

Huntington was correct to note the role of religious and cultural elements, but, as a universal explanation for geopolitics, his account was inadequate. Religion made scant sense of divisions in East Asia, particularly between North and South Korea, and China and Japan, unless leadership cults and governing ideologies were seen to have religious characteristics.

Moreover, in terms of Islam and Christianity, rivalries within each bloc, for example, Shia versus Sunni and (to a lesser extent) Protestant versus Catholic, could be as serious and bloody, or more so, than those between blocs. In Iraq and Syria in the 2010s, the Islamic State (ISIS) movement was to make this bloodily apparent. In turn, the determination of ISIS to create a theocratic government took precedence over existing national boundaries. As such, ISIS and similar movements threw geopolitics to the fore in terms of expounding a different basis for a territorial sway. This also influenced the parameters of the response. The United States eventually played a significant role in confronting ISIS but found it difficult to pursue a consistent policy in the face of contrasting political situations in Iraq and Syria, as well as regional partners who had their own views and regarded US inconsistency with considerable wariness.[10] How far this was a matter for geopolitical understanding other than in the important terms of the differences between Iraq and Syria and the distribution of ethnic and sectarian groups, notably Kurds, is unclear.

What is more valuable is the assessment of how far the geopolitics of this episode and others depended on whether the state or movement in question was on the rise/attack/offensive (and these are not coterminous) or on the opposite.[11] Moreover, as with the issue of whether Karl Marx's very analysis possibly altered the prospect for the process he discussed, so the very envisaging of a geopolitical threat might either make it one (in part by the response) or ensure its failure.

At the same time, Huntington was significant because he proposed a new geopolitical thesis to explain global developments. There was a common fault in the drive for a global span, whereas with geopolitics it is reasonable to assume that any analysis would be more geospecific in its application: in some areas rather than others. That might strike some as an unscientific proposal and one that is more impressionistic than mathematically precise. Yet such a proposal is more acutely observant of the variations of the world than one that seeks to reduce it to system whatever this system might mean.

The war on terror and the Iraq War of 2003 meant that Huntington's thesis was still much discussed, but its relevance appeared of scant value for or to China and Russia. Arguably, Western commentators paid far too little attention to their pronouncements, and that despite the degree to which they were less opaque than had been the case during the Cold War. Thus, on February 10, 2007, Vladimir Putin at the Munich Security Council, decried a unipolar world in which the United States felt free to act as it wished. He held out an alternative of a multipolarity based on "new centres of global economic growth." Putin specifically complained about NATO's eastward expansion and concerning the extension of US missile defenses. It is not necessary to agree (or disagree) with Putin's points and policy to note the importance of his views. Furthermore, their tone is instructive, notably his paranoia. This is significant for geopolitics as a whole: it concerns tone as much as content. Together they constitute the substance of geopolitics, and each rests in large part on the psychological dimensions of the strategic culture of individual countries, or at least key elements within them.

In the case of Putin, there is a shared concern with Xi Jinping in supporting "national rejuvenation." For each, there is a historical dimension to the geopolitics, that of a past compromising of position due to hostile outside forces. This was a geopolitics that centered on past territorial and prestige losses, more recently so for Russia than for China, and the geopolitics very much focused on nearby zones of should-be control, with the "should" resting on history and assertion and denying change and democratic mandate. NATO was particularly contentious due to its geographical range, including to the borders of Russia as well as US membership. It is far from alone as a regional organization that has geopolitical significance. Others include the Shanghai Cooperation Organisation established in 2001, the Gulf Cooperation Council that intervened in Bahrain in 2011, and the Economic Community of West African States. Far, however, from these being compatible or even linkable, in a form of a global system of cooperative organizations,[12] there is an ad hoc character to the organizations and their relationship.

The very flexibility of the concept of geopolitics ensured that it was applied freely. It also had an authority that led to frequent use in the literature on international relations. *Sea Power* (2017) by James Stavridis, a retired US admiral, was typical in having *The History and Geopolitics of the World's Oceans* as its subtitle. In practice, the book was really about the United States and used familiar ideas, such as choke points, to argue for what were presented as geopolitical realities. Ironically, the extent to which such choke points required reinterpretation in terms of air-sea potential was one that made this idea of "realities" inherently transient. *Geopolitics* was a frequent term in journalism, as in the *New York Times* of July 17, 2023, when analyzing changing demographic structures: "The world's demographics are changing. . . . The best-balanced work forces will mostly be in South and Southeast Asia, Africa and the Middle East, according to U.N. projections, potentially reshaping economic growth and geopolitical power balances." Again for China in 2023: "Indeed, the rise of an economically powerful, authoritarian China presents the geopolitical challenge of the century."[13]

The very flexibility of concepts and of their usage helped ensure that commentators and others could readily find ammunition for their views. This process was also seen in divisions between policymakers, although the latter scarcely required geopolitical differences. This, for example, was seen with the serious differences affecting the US policy in the Iraq crisis of 2003, not least the rivalry between the Department of Defense and the State Department. There was a geographical component in the sense of relations with Iran, but this, and certainly its geographical dimension, was not the prime issue nor means of discussion.

More broadly, and both between and within states, due to the demise of revolutionary Communism, ideologies three decades into the twenty-first century are much weaker than in the Cold War, and certainly so as far as the contrast between the United States and China are concerned. Moreover, nonaligned countries' defense expenditures are far higher than in the past, as also is their share of global GDP.[14] This is part of a rapidly changing world that provides a changing dynamic for geopolitics. Although the US has benefited from support from sovereign wealth funds, as in the fiscal crisis of 2007,[15] the weakness of the dollar, certainly in terms of international acceptability, challenges the current fiscal world system. However defined, the stable international monetary order is highly vulnerable at present.

The contrast with the past is readily apparent. At Bretton Woods in 1944, it was possible to create a new international fiscal system easing capital and trade flows in part due to the destruction of the previous system in the Depression and World War II. The United States was able to dominate the forty-four participants.[16] In a more multipolar world, this dominance is no longer the case, and hostile powers increased the costs inherent to a dollar-dominated financial system.

SEVEN

THE GEOPOLITICS
OF THE PRESENT
Ideas and Realities

GEOPOLITICS WERE MUCH PUSHED TO the fore from the start of the century, as the difficulties facing intervention in Afghanistan and Iraq were followed by the apparent revival of great-power competition. The latter was accentuated in 2022 by the Russian invasion of Ukraine and the Chinese threat to Taiwan. These led to general claims of the significance of geography and thus geopolitics and more specific use of both to explain particular policies and debate threats.

Unsurprisingly, this revival was not accompanied by any clarification of the conceptual issues involved. In particular, there was the difficulty of distinguishing between the descriptive and prescriptive usage of geopolitical ideas, the issue of resolving the relationships between geopolitical factors at different spatial scales, and the question of what were the prime factors to be assessed when power, effectiveness, and other elements were considered in geopolitical terms. The last was highlighted in the successive crises of the last quarter century, notably regarding whether there were strategic interests involved for major international powers in several, especially Kosovo and Afghanistan, or, linked to that, how best these interests should be discussed. None of these questions were new, but they served in each period to emphasize that geopolitics was a practice of thought rather than a set of answers and a sphere and scale for strategies and operations, not a doctrine. The amorphous character of *geopolitics* as a term emerges clearly. At the same time, there were shifts in emphasis as to which geography was at stake and how best to assess it.

As before, these issues were complicated by the number of actors involved, whether national, supranational, or subnational, as well as the degree to which each could appear very different from particular perspectives. Thus, the international interoperability that the United States sought from its allies, notably in Europe[1] and East Asia, has only limited meaning in terms of these putative allies. They place the emphasis on their own interests. Like the US, whose commentators are apt to forget or underplay the point and its consequences, these allies have their own commitments, exigencies, and, as it were, geopolitics. In particular, the need on the part of allies for domestic stability and internal security poses military and political demands that may be of limited interest to the United States with its level of geopolitical concern and interest. Looked at differently, each state understands its own domestic politics, including geopolitics, but not that of other states. So also with geopolitical and geoeconomic tensions within alliance or would-be alliance systems, for example, between Japan and South Korea or Britain and the European Union.

The very failure of outside commentators to understand such tensions contributes to their seriously flawed geopolitical vision, conceptualization, and reasoning. Moreover, the very variety in the possible descriptive terms that can be applied indicates the number of approaches that can be taken as each of these terms have very different resonances. In particular, global geopolitical analyses are apt to underrate ideologies, values, domestic factors, and specific national interests, as with the war between Argentina and Britain over the Falkland Islands in 1982. This greatly worried US commentators, who did not wish to see NATO assets going to the bottom of the South Atlantic.

By the early 2020s, there had been a reemphasis on economic zones of production as opposed to strategic points of control. This reflected the extent to which points of control took on meaning in part through determining access to areas of economic activity. Moreover, the impact of the latter on military strength was of greater importance as the real as well as nominal cost of this strength rose greatly, which it did in the 2010s and then 2020s. Military investment shot up, which led to arms races that reflected domestic economic and governmental strength. This rise was a marked contrast to the situation in the 1990s when there was the combination of serious fiscal and economic disruption for many states, notably Russia, and the "peace dividend" of expenditure cuts for Western powers. Both showed the need to contextualize what is understood as geopolitics, or, rather, its open-ended character as a habit of thought. Moreover, the geopolitics of the 1990s thereby had a "permissive" character for the United States and its allies.

At any rate, the geopolitics of the 1990s was made more diffuse by the global range of humanitarian concerns enunciated by Western leaders, a range that stretched from Kosovo to East Timor. In response, there appeared to be a lack of strategic and geopolitical clarity. Alongside the resulting sense of failure, a particular strategic crisis was discerned in specific circumstances, as for the US Navy, which apparently lacked a function in the 1990s and 2000s.[2]

Turning to 2022–24, the Ukraine crisis led to much discussion of how far resources explained Russia's attempt at annexation and, more specifically, whether there was a key drive to control much of the world's export of grain, not least with the international influence that this could bring. Russia and Ukraine together produce 30 percent of the world's trade in wheat and large quantities of that in barley and maize.[3] This offered an ability of sustaining challenge and influence internationally, notably in African countries dependent on grain imports, such as Egypt. As with the explanation of US policy in the Middle East beginning in the late twentieth century, and more specifically regarding Iraq in 2003, in terms of oil, this approach, however, left out much.

Moreover, grain exports provide Ukraine with a source of revenue and economic value that are important in sustaining its economy and reducing its need for Western financial support. Such an outcome is part of the geopolitics of the war because, with the failure of the initial Russian plan, Ukraine became an extension of the West but one that was therefore subject to the attritional pressures that Russia sought to apply. Whereas in Ukraine these were kinetic, in the West these pressures were a matter of economic and political dislocation, including high rates of inflation. These were not simply a product of the supply and cost of raw materials, but these were important to the equation.

More specifically, this situation underlined the importance of the Black Sea coast of Ukraine. Whereas grain is produced across a significant area that therefore poses issues of control, the storage, processing, and shipping of grain is concentrated on the ports. Moreover, the limitations, notably limited flexibility, of the rail system made the rapid substitution by new routes difficult, although, as an important aspect of the geopolitics of the war, there was a shift to different methods. Aside from rail and road links to the West, this also involved the use of river ports on the Danube. In 2023, Lithuania suggested that the EU should invest in a route from Poland to the Baltic ports to handle Ukraine's grain.

In turn, Russia applied power to enforce its blockade, not least by deploying warships, by mining coastal waters, and by drone attacks. Control over territory has a very different meaning at sea, being inherently more transient once ports are taken out of the equation. Maps may depict an apparent shaping of control provided by weapon range, and this has been accentuated by the capability of missile systems, as with Baltic vulnerability to missiles based in Kaliningrad.

At the same time, as with every level of geopolitics, from the global to the local, the strategic to the tactical, there is a development and deployment of opposing practices and systems designed to lessen and counter geopolitical capabilities. The most significant at the global level are balance of power and containment practices and systems. At the operational level, the Ukraine conflict saw the attack on command posts, communication facilities, notably bridges, and supply facilities, all of which were designed to counter the advantages of opponents.

The range of missiles took on renewed geopolitical significance during the Ukraine war as it had not done in recent conflicts in, for example, Ethiopia, Myanmar, and Sudan because of speculation about the possible Russian use of nuclear weaponry and due to the capabilities of hypersonic missiles. The latter, moreover, were to the fore in discussion about a possible US-Chinese clash over Taiwan. Such a clash and, indeed, the initial Russian plans for Ukraine brought to the fore another aspect of geopolitics, one that tends to receive insufficient attention—namely, the time sequence. Gaining geopolitical advantage can take a variety of forms, from the seizure of territory to the deployment of weapon systems denying access to opponents. All of these have more weight if done rapidly and therefore within the opponents' perception-decision-action cycle. In effect, the latter is disrupted, thwarted, and, in part, suppressed as a consequence of rapidity. Thus, speed provides a geopolitical advantage that cannot be assessed simply in terms of space. Gaining control of the time sequence provides an escalation dominance akin to that of the psychological mastery offered by trumping through the use of threats, notably nuclear ones.

Aside from grain, other traditional raw materials remain significant. Thus, in 2022, helped by the US investment in fracking, as well as the continued Chinese reliance on coal, fossil fuels still provided about four-fifths of the global consumption of energy. Although there were significant energy efficiencies in industrial processes, there was still massive and growing global demand for energy, in part due to rising population and linked to expectations about economic activity and living standards. This demand helped ensure that energy provision and security were important to global power politics.

Yet, as a reminder of the need to put the "geo" of place in context, a variety of factors was involved in the availability of energy. A key one was capital and the rate at which it was available. Thus, the low interest rates of the 2010s facilitated new initiatives, such as fracking and green energy. Public policy in the shape of responses to climate change may provide another form of geopolitics, as with China's success in creating a major solar panel industry.[4]

It was no accident that energy supplies provided context, conjuncture, and contingency for the Ukraine crisis. In particular, the European reliance on Russian gas supplies was taken as an explanation for German ambivalence about opposing Russia. Moreover, the destruction in 2022 of the major trans-Baltic Nord Stream 1 and 2 pipelines taking gas to Western Europe (Nord Stream 2 had not yet begun operation) was an important military step, albeit one shrouded in secrecy and thus deniability. This step, like the use of threats of nuclear attack or the possibility of severing subsea cables, was an instance of the range of hybrid warfare seen in the conflict. Whatever the language, this range was scarcely new. However, it brought to the fore the extent to which conflict both involved control over territory, in this case Ukraine, and entailed factors that were far less "territorial." Notable among the latter was the psychological manipulation that was intended to provide reflexive control, in part by offering an image of strength while weakening purpose elsewhere.

The environmental dynamics of economic change further led to a concern about the availability of the materials, notably cobalt and lithium, that would be important for the production of relevant technology. This would create a new geopolitics of interest.[5] There was strong Western concern about the Chinese ability to take control of much of this material. Indeed, Chinese geopolitics in Africa were in part understood in these terms.

Separately, the relevance of ideas and knowledge-creation "spaces," society, and practices to geopolitics in turn is unclear. The very value of the digital economy as well as its locational activity appear highly dependent on stock market shifts and other aspects of profitability and valuation, rather than classic geopolitical factors.

More specifically, the geographical terminology generally employed arises from geopolitical concerns, as with the use of *Indo-Pacific* to describe a region that in practice is difficult to define. It is unclear whether this region is supposed to reach to California and Cape Town or has a more circumscribed span. It is also unclear how far this region is an ad hoc response to particular needs, notably cooperation against China and, indeed, competition with it. The latter is the focus of the US Indo-Pacific Command, which reaches to the west coast of India rather than to Cape Town.

Whatever this individual case, however, discussed in terms of regions, zones, and the active processes involved in discerning both, the character of geopolitics is made more dynamic by changes in weapons technology, including that of the relevant platforms. This point was understood when Mackinder discussed the matter in 1904. Weapons on the whole have a tactical impact and, looked at differently, an impact that helps make conflict local, as with the glaciation of the war in Ukraine starting late 2022. At the same time, as Mackinder argued, the impact, indeed possible consequences, of the deployment, even use, of weapons can have not only operational consequences but also strategic ones. The latter are inseparable from geopolitics at the global level. A classic instance is provided by the deployment of missile systems by China and their threat to a US Pacific geopolitics that owed much to carriers. Indeed, the latter underpinned the US alliance system for it was the belief that the United States could provide effective support that offered security guarantees to Japan, South Korea, Taiwan, the Philippines, and other allies. The possibility that this support could be rapidly removed by, as it were, a more deadly Pearl Harbor or surprise attack, provoked much discussion about a strategic and, thereby, geopolitical shift against the US.

In 1941, the United States had two key classes of warship, the battleship and the carrier, and damage to the former class still left crucial carriers at sea. In 2023, the key classes are the carrier and the nuclear-armed submarine. The potential of the latter for a subnuclear war, however, is unclear, not least given assumed ideological and doctrinal restraints on the escalation to a nuclear conflict. Moreover, hostile powers are deploying more effective antisubmarine technology, with Russia allegedly providing China with much that the latter seeks. The extent to which fleets or, indeed, individual carrier-led units are geopolitical features raises questions about the durability of such a feature. Clearly, major naval squadrons have a greater ability to project, deploy, and use power than many individual states. How far they should be seen as platforms equivalent to states or otherwise conceptualized in geopolitical terms, however, is unclear. Moreover, the ability of modest weapons, such as mines or torpedoes, to destroy these platforms further raises issues of definition.

Discussion of geopolitics in terms of developing military technologies serves as a reminder that this is a continuous theme in the subject. In particular, those who write about geopolitics tend to be most interested in power and change and, therefore, present military developments as a measure of both. This may be mistaken if it leads to a downplaying of the significance as well of economic factors, which, separately, have become more important with the cost of new weapon systems and the apparent need to replace existing ones. Obsolescence therefore in part is a measure of geopolitical pressure, as also happened with the introduction of new dreadnought-type battleships from the mid-1900s and of effective aircraft carriers from the 1930s.

All these factors, however, underrate the quality of geopolitical perception and leadership and, linked to this, the ability to understand and respond to situations. There is only limited information about the nature, character, and skill of geopolitical conceptualization and implementation in most countries, notably China. There is also scant sign that Western geopolitical assessment is particularly skillful. This is one way of assessing the difficulties of establishing prioritization in strategic terms. The lack of any clear intellectual or practical distinction between geopolitics and strategy helps ensure that it is possible to relate failure in one to that in the other.

Whether this is better or worse than the situation in other periods invites consideration. Certainly, the lack of any central theme comparable to that of the Cold War provides an opportunity to consider the difficulties of translating geopolitical assumptions into the multifaceted refractions of a complex world, with many international actors motivated by a range of drives that are difficult to reduce to any consistent assessment or to present in terms of a central theme.

While the specific playing out of rivalry in terms of maritime access issues was highly geopolitical, the psychological dimensions of international politics were to the fore in some well-received accounts of Sino-US rivalry and its possible consequences. This was particularly the case with Graham Allison's *Destined for War: Can America and China Escape Thucydides's Trap?* (Boston, 2017). As with most historical modeling, this was not geopolitical in its inherent character, instead focusing on the relationship between rising and declining powers. More particularly, such modeling proved an easier way to discuss the Sino-US rivalry as a whole rather than with reference to the often hidden specifics of the moment. Alongside the rising and declining theme, there was also that of the rivalry between autocratic and democratic powers,[6] with China moreover being attuned to a move toward authoritarianism in Asia and actively assisting the process in Cambodia and Myanmar.[7] Proximity to China is a factor in the promotion and support of authoritarian goals.[8]

The tendency in geopolitical commentary to treat states as monoliths draws on a range of characteristics including the idea that the strategic culture of individual states leads in that direction. States can then be labeled, notably as rising or declining, or as maritime or continental powers, the latter recently by Sarah

Paine.[9] There is the confirmation bias of institutional interest in this specific case, with Paine being a long-standing chair at the US Naval War College. Moreover, such arguments offer a form of determinism that is not only intellectually suspect, especially in assuming a degree of consistency,[10] but also prone to lead to a misunderstanding of the policies and capabilities of particular states at specific moments.

This misunderstanding is notably directed at states with contrasting ideologies and, more generally so, if the other state is authoritarian and thus prone to present what might appear misleading accounts of its intentions. First, at the level of all other states, it is instructive that commentators, while allowing for division and complexity in the politics and policymaking of their own state, generally do not do so when discussing other states or present them in terms of a relatively simple dualism, with one tendency being desirable and the other not so. Moreover, as an aspect of the latter, external alignment can be pushed to the fore, as with the argument that the dualism is explained accordingly, for example, pro-US or pro-Soviet.

Clarity in explanation is another way of looking at simplicity and over-confidence, and the "geography as destiny" position very much exemplifies this. In practice, however, there are tendencies within governments, and these can be greatly affected by international and domestic interactions.

So also with the idea that timing provides a form of inevitability, as in the Germans had to attack in World War I before French-financed Russian rail development changed the timetable for Russian military mobilization. An alternative would have explained why Israel attacked

Iran in 2011–23 before its atomic capability was built up or the United States did likewise with North Korea in the same period. Obviously neither occurred, which serves as a reminder of the folly of arguing for inevitability but also the ease with which it can be advanced.

The idea of monolithic power intentions was applied by critics, international and domestic, to the United States during the Cold War and subsequently. It drew on the realities of US strength and a strong degree of bipartisanship in the definition of security interests and support for them. Yet it was readily apparent that there were also significant differences in US policymaking. These encompassed political, economic, and military interests and policies. Thus, in 2001–12, while many policymakers and much of the army were committed to conflict linked to the war on terror, in practice a reification of a series of disparate challenges, the navy was emphasizing the need for a "pivot to Asia," in the sense of a challenge from China, and was war gaming accordingly.

In turn, this challenge can be differently assessed. The rise of a great power does not necessarily lead to conflict with the existing hegemon, as Anglo-US relations demonstrated from 1815 to the 1950s. Moreover, the concept, in that case, of spheres of interest scarcely did justice to continued and largely untroubled British territories in the Caribbean, North America, and the Pacific. The extent to which the rising power perceives openness and fairness in the response to it is important to its behavior.[11]

With China, there has been very different rhetorical and other "mood music" about intentions, policies, and capabilities to the case of, say, Britain. Assertion is clearly very significant, with a "near China" that is seen as within a desired sphere of control, as well as the determination not to let the United States intervene. Yet, in policy terms, this does not set a particular agenda. There are a host of variables, including the unpredictable consequences of any clash set off by North Korean actions. There is also the "learning process" of refracted experience, in this case the difficulties Russia encountered in Ukraine. The extent to which this might act as a template for Taiwan is unclear but is a reminder that one element of geopolitical analysis ought to be the frame of reference employed by contemporaries in comparisons. This frame can be historical, geographical, or both, but again, determinism is inappropriate for there is no necessary linkage or analysis. Thus, at present, Ukraine dominates attention as a comparative marker, but there have also been conflicts in 2022–23 in Ethiopia, Myanmar, and Sudan. Moreover, Taiwan, an island that can be blockaded, is very different from Ukraine as a geomilitary target and sphere for operations. In addition, over Ukraine, there was already an immediate history of conflict going back to the Soviet seizure of Crimea in 2014.

A threat environment does not determine the response. In part, this environment has its own weaknesses and frictions. Russia in the early 2020s was revealed as having dysfunctional governance and a divided elite. Very differently, China's attempt to create a new geoeconomic order through its Belt and Road Initiative and thereby to cement geopolitical influence has hit repeated problems in terms of local viability, responses, and stability. The lack of an underlying economic and political logic for many of the projects compares with weaknesses for particular British and US initiatives over the past two centuries, but, arguably, failure in China's case has been more abrupt due to the determination to surpass normal market considerations. At any rate, as with the impact on British interests of nationalization policies in the twentieth century, from Mexico to Egypt, so China's global geopolitics looks more impressive as a map of schemes rather than as an account of implementation.

Unsurprisingly, Xi Jinping told President Mauricio Macri of Argentina in 2017 that Latin America was the natural extension of the maritime silk road that China was trying to establish. Yet that scarcely establishes priority. So also in July 2023 when President Raisi of Iran sought to develop alliances with Kenya, Uganda, and Zimbabwe, the latter two of which had clashes with the United States, including the imposition or threat of sanctions.

China has been helped greatly by its peaceful relations with Russia in recent decades and by the fact that neither India nor Vietnam are really in a position to do harm. Moreover, Tibet and Xinjiang can be controlled by Chinese security forces without a significant counter-insurgency effort. As a result, China is able to focus on naval buildup, maritime power projection, and confrontation with the United States in the western Pacific. This is very different from the emphasis of Japanese expansionism in the 1930s or indeed of Soviet and later Russian activity from its Pacific bases. Japan focused, instead, on China, and the Soviet Union, later Russia, essentially on European commitments. Afghanistan in 1979–89 was an outlier.

The situation of China, a geopolitics by default as it were, has allowed China a margin of freedom and provided it with the opportunity to pursue with the United

States a one-front confrontation, which has been the geo-strategic goal of all powers. The equivalent is that of the US in 1917 as it needed only to fight Germany. Moreover, China anyway is better able to cope with this situation because of its economic growth and its only limited need for manufactured imports.

However, less positive is the geopolitical fact that China is faced by powers that look to the United States for their security, notably Taiwan, Japan, South Korea, and the Philippines. In contrast, the US, when it rose, did not have to face a comparable situation after the 1860s, for France abandoned its commitment in Mexico and Britain successfully sought to settle issues with the United States, which it did by the Treaty of Washington in 1871.

That other powers besides the United States oppose Chinese expansionism helps the US by complicating this expansionism, but also provides an alliance vulnerability and commitment pressure that challenge US strategic freedom. Geopolitical strength, in terms of the counting of resources, therefore, does not necessarily equate with the necessarily flexibility of choice that is important to the assessment of geopolitical problems and possibilities. The domestic pressures that await what might be perceived as a climbdown complicate this, as well as the more general systemic criticism of any failure to support allies. All these points underline the continuing theme in this book of the role of perception and place of subjectivity in the contemporary and subsequent understanding of geopolitical issues and actions. As an additional factor, real and possible allies, as well as declared neutrals, can show considerable autonomy that is both potentially weakening and throws an emphasis on the perception of consistency.[12]

Thus, geopolitics is commonly understood territorially, but in contrast, in terms of struggles between states, it can also relate to political purpose and the range of political methods that are used. This provides a way to understand what has been described as "hybrid warfare," with particular reference to the means employed by the Russians in 2014 to take Crimea from Ukraine. In practice, these methods rest on a doctrine in which geopolitics is understood as central to rivalries that encompass a spectrum, including the military side of conflict and economic, political, and propaganda aspects. Moreover, this approach collapses any distinction between international and domestic control.[13]

EIGHT

—✺—

INTO THE FUTURE

Apparent security should not tempt us to forget that new enemies and unknown dangers may *possibly* arise from some obscure people, scarcely visible in the map of the world. The Arabs or Saracens, who spread their conquests from India to Spain, had languished in poverty and contempt till Mahomet breathed into those savage bodies that soul of enthusiasm.

Edward Gibbon, *Decline and Fall*

THE EXTENSION OF GEOPOLITICS INTO space began with rockets able to move out of the Earth's atmosphere. This extension was crystallized by the apparent possibilities offered by a presence in space, notably for surveillance and weaponry, and by the prospect of the extraction of minerals. Thus, in 2022, a Chinese lunar test mission discovered Changesite-(Y), a new phosphate mineral that could be used as fuel for nuclear fusion. The composition of the moon indeed includes large amounts of alumina, iron, magnesia, and titanium. This potential helped make space warfare of immediate interest, as did the drive to protect and threaten surveillance and communications capabilities. Dedicated space command branches of the military have been or are being established by a number of states including the United States, Australia, Britain, France, and Germany.

The role of satellites was highlighted in the Ukraine war with Russian hacking attempts thwarted by the provision of US satellite assistance to the Ukrainian military. A key role was played by Elon Musk through his Space X's Starlink. By mid-2023, Musk had over 3,500 satellites in orbit, thus providing mass of a new form. In turn, Russia tested electronic warfare systems aimed at US satellites, notably by jamming them and by the potential use of anti-satellite missiles able to hit targets orbiting at 17,500 miles per hour, which, moreover, would produce debris able to damage other satellites, as with a test in 2021 when a defunct Soviet satellite, Cosmos 1408, was destroyed. The United States, China, and India all also have antisatellite weaponry.

Developing technology, in this case in the shape of satellites and antisatellite weaponry, poses problems for thinking about and depicting geopolitics, including the continual potency of particular geographical elements as well as the opportunities provided by these developments. The most obvious problems militarily arise in protecting the very systems that offer opportunities, but there are also the issues involved not only in using information but also in understanding the relevant issues and appropriate processes. All of these have been the case throughout the practice of geopolitics, at whatever level, but the speed of development now poses difficulties.

The deployment, use, and protection of relevant material in an appropriate time sequence has always been an issue for understanding spatial relationships in capability and, more particularly, conflict. At present, real-time mapping means not the hasty assimilation of visual reconnaissance by an observer in the field, but the closure of the gap between surveillance, decision, and firing system, as automated processes and digital location are employed. However, the prospect of such mapping being affected by attacks on communication systems, whether satellites or computers, threatens to plunge opponents into a cartographic, indeed information, void. Thus, the very enhanced capability that appeared to stem from cartographic improvement and application also threatened a vulnerability that was far greater in air reconnaissance assets than in the two world wars and the Cold War.

Geographical information can be provided now from drones and, locally, microdrones. These and other technological changes, past, present, and future, can offer an enhanced possibility for the implementation of a geopolitics, with the latter understood as a politics present in spatial terms and explained through it. It is difficult, however, to assess how cyber capabilities will affect geopolitics, not least as they appear to have the ability to overcome distance. At the same time, these capabilities cannot provide for the occupation of territory. Moreover, their kinetic possibilities are very limited.

Politics take on energy by exposition and discussion. In this, it is difficult to know what the building blocks of rhetorical geopolitics will be in the future, what in short will replace "Munich," "Suez," "Cuba," "Vietnam," "Iraq," "Afghanistan," and others. Clearly, the references will vary by state, as has hitherto been the case. Particular goals can be sought with the use of geopolitical arguments, as in July 2023 when President Nauseda of Lithuania pressed for permanent NATO defensive bases near Russia's eastern borders, in place of a 1997 treaty with Russia prohibiting them under "current security circumstances," on the grounds, he argued, that Russian policy had essentially destroyed the agreement. In a guest article appearing in the *Frankfurter Allgemeine Zeitung* on July 10, Nauseda argued that a successful Russian advance would expose Germany, as in 1760, 1920, and 1945. The last, when Hitler was overthrown, was not the happiest of comparisons.

The use of historical examples may be less defined by a duality than was the case, at least in theory, during the Cold War. Indeed, the international reaction to the Russian invasion of Ukraine proved salutary to the West in this respect because many more states sought neutrality than had been anticipated. Moreover, the geopolitical markers were not those sought by Western commentators. Thus, on the pattern of Cold War exchanges, US criticism of the Russian invasion of Ukraine were frequently met in "nonaligned countries," such as South Africa, by reference to the US invasion of Iraq in 2003. This comparison indicated the simultaneity of the rhetoric of geopolitics, as well as its unfixed nature in terms of the place of reference. The future will therefore create a new present (and past). The political resentments of the Global South include what was presented as unfairness, even exploitation, by Western governments and companies in the response to the COVID pandemic. Radicals assume that the pressure for social and ecological revolution will have a geopolitical dimension, being concentrated in the Southern Hemisphere or beginning there.[1]

Moreover, the perceptions bound up in geopolitics are inherently in a state of flux and to a degree that clashes markedly with the language about fixity of interests—"geography as destiny"—that is so frequently deployed. This observation might appear to represent a critique of "the public," but perceptions are also at play for political actors and military planners. In part, this is an obvious consequence of the range of activity that has to be engaged. Thus, what geopolitics means in the context of "triphibious" warfare and "cross-domain synergy" is not immediately apparent. Political actors are more generally involved in a situation in which major uncertainty is inherent in decision-making. Yet again, this is an instructive contrast to the apparent fixity of geopolitics. Indeed, commentators in 2023 felt able to counterpoint particular geopolitical interpretations from the past when discussing the present situation, while also employing the resonant vocabulary of the subject. A sense of the immediate present taking precedence, which was the opposite of the standard interpretation of geopolitics, was captured by the distinguished historian Niall Ferguson in his Bloomberg column of July 2, 2023, one in which geopolitics was also presented in a diachronic fashion:

> Today's geopolitics and economics have more in common with the 17th century than the 20th. . . . What is the wider significance of the crisis in Russia? Two weeks ago, I warned that the geopolitics of Cold War seemed to be pitting Halford J. Mackinder's vast Eurasian "Heartland" against Nicholas J. Spykman's "Rimland." If the Heartland consists of a new "Axis" of China, Russia and Iran, the Rimland is the coalition the US has formed with its European and Asian allies to support Ukraine. But I worried that the Rimland

was showing signs of division. The Prigozhin mutiny seems to have proved them right. Maybe it's the Heartland, not the Rimland, that is cracking up.[2]

Aside from the continuity of terms, which is characteristic of the use of geopolitical arguments, it is striking how far the standard geographical focus on Eurasia continues to leave out much of the world, more particularly Africa and South America.[3] This relates both to the discussion of them and to the geopolitical arguments advanced. There could be a highly explicit linkage between events and discussion, as with Augusto Pinochet, military dictator of Chile in 1973–90, who had been professor of geopolitics and subdirector at the Chilean War Academy when he published *Geopolíca* (1968). This drew on a tradition of interest in the subject, with Pinochet succeeding to the chair held by General Gregorio Rodríguez Tascón, who worked on geopolitics. Such work, however, does not tend to be incorporated into the set intellectual pedigree, cast, and agenda of geopolitics, which, in this respect, is similar to strategy having such a restriction.

The content and character of strategic thought in Africa deserves even more attention as, with Asia, it is the continent that has seen the most conflict since World War II. How far, and how, that conflict is understood in geopolitical terms by African leaders deserves far more attention than it receives at a time of the standard subject *menage à trois* of the United States, China, and Russia. In particular, challenges in Africa that cross state boundaries, such as that of fundamentalist Islam in the Sahel belt south of the Sahara, deserve consideration, but in more specific terms than "war between civilizations." For example, the conflicts in the Horn of Africa, involving the states from Sudan to Congo and their neighbors, exemplify the process of "the foe of my foe is my friend," which is an essential form of geopolitical thought when it has a spatial setting.

Environmental considerations will affect the geopolitics of the future. Yet, far from this being a clear-cut process, there will be a series of developments, some at cross-purposes. Moreover, "ownership" of the relevant geopolitics will vary greatly, depending on which group is being considered: the geopolitics of environmental change will vary not only by country but also by the group surveyed.

The relevant environment includes that of military technology, but here again there will be variety. Thus, in terms of the application of AI to bulk-data analysis, major powers will be able to apply their systems to identify targets, and this will give them enhanced capability, notably so in conjunction with hypersonic missiles. The United States and China will probably be best able to direct resources to that end, for example, in tracking and targeting hostile submarines. However, while very valuable at the operational level, AI will not provide a strategic tool capable of replacing established attributes of political and military leadership at that level. Furthermore, the operational effectiveness of AI will be greater in certain milieux and for particular weapon systems than for others. In particular, it will be more effective at sea, where there are a finite number of targets, rather than on land, where conflict in cities is a particular problem. Large maritime targets, such as aircraft carriers, will be especially vulnerable. Indeed, it will probably be most appropriate to put maritime targets such as maritime aircraft in protected bases rather than at sea.

However, as with most aspects of present and future geopolitics, it will only be possible to establish the nature of this capability under the shock of conflict and the risk, uncertainty, and depreciation it entails. This makes not only prediction difficult but also extrapolating from one episode to another. For example, it is unlikely that cyber warfare will replace its kinetic counterpart.[4] There are also psychological assumptions bound up in weapon systems choices, as with the continued preference for manned flight, and to a degree, that reflects historical ideas about masculinity rather than the practicality of using unmanned flight in many contexts or, rather, with the manned component at the level of distant control.

The ability and willingness of major powers to invest in full-spectrum capabilities will also vary. For the United States, the danger emerges more clearly because China is and will be more powerful in economic terms and able to react more speedily to developments and possibilities than was the Soviet Union. Thus, Chinese shipbuilding capacity is far greater than that of the US, allegedly by July 2023 about 232 times greater according to the Office of Naval Intelligence.[5] The Soviet Union, in contrast, proved especially poor in adapting to the new technological possibilities of the 1980s, notably the spread of information systems and the greater use of computers. In turn, Chinese adaptability appears to some also to be speedier in comparison with the United States, not least because in the US there is greater emphasis on living standards and social welfare expenditure, while taxation is relatively low. Again, geopolitics has to take note of politics.

Whether the United States can compete, as claimed, by virtue of the innovative range permitted by limited central control is unclear, however much it accords with Western ideological ideas, not least because there is the issue of applying this range to military procurement and deployment. How far this will or should lead to "America first" policies in place of collective defense is unclear. There is the argument that to do so reduces risk and expense for the United States and increases autonomy.[6] There is also the problem that if, following the precepts of Donald Trump and lessening or abandoning commitments to allies, the latter, in turn, will also become more transactional in their relations. This weakens the United States' ability to portray itself as in geopolitical control of a unified bloc. As a result, a balance of power politics is harder to pursue. Transactional relations also put pressure on the wider economic interchange that brings significant systemic benefit.

Looking to the future may involve "blue skies" outcomes in the shape of a "black skies" nothingness. However, aside from the prospect of major environmental change, for example, the danger that the Atlantic Meridional Overturning Circulation would shut down, ending the Gulf Stream, there is also the possibility of a disastrous interaction with an extrasolar element. This may be one that causes environmental cataclysm and disease or, alternatively, a more focused hostility, as currently in the field of fiction, rather as was the equivalent of atomic power, for example, in Agatha Christie's *The Big Four* (1927). This, nevertheless, presents the chance of a geopolitics influenced, even determined, by very different forces to those employed hitherto. Geopolitical models tend to use rational explanations of interests and goals, but the rationality in question may be very different, indeed, to borrow the phrase by Samuel Huntington, one of the form of a clash of civilizations. In this, as in other cases, motivating drives can be treated as rational, but the rationality may be that of a Darwinian body needing fulfillment in organic terms rather than a cerebral mind. What will geopolitics mean for robots?

To move from outer space in an unclear timespan to the Earth in the near future may appear mundane but is a reminder of the degree to which it is foolish to assume any particular direction of flow or priority in the formulation and discussion of geopolitics. This is more generally the case given the problem posed by the failure to make explicit this point and, indeed, similar conceptual and methodological issues.

The Earth today is, as with all other todays, a moment in time between past and future, and the latter is inevitably included within the planning and speculation of the present. Unsurprisingly, there is much that is well-established in both. Indeed, whether in terms of the prospect of rivalry between China and the United States or Russia, the potential impact of rocketry, and the choices that may be made by the Global South, we are essentially still in the continuity of a period that really began in the 1950s and was brought to the fore in the (late) 1960s, in part with the relative decline of Western power.

The emphasis to be placed on each element, however, varies, as does its interactive character. Thus, in the early 1970s, as it proved difficult for the United States to extricate itself from the Vietnam commitment and contain the consequences of failure, so the crisis in Chinese-Soviet relations provided fundamental opportunities for the Nixon government. More notably, these opportunities were sustained by its successors until the 1990s, the loss then of the political alignment proving a major mistake for the United States but not for a China that no longer required a security guarantee against Russia.

In the early 2020s, there appears to be no such possibility as Russian and Chinese expansionism are both opposed by the United States. Yet that leaves unclear both the possible consequences of political and economic tensions, if not rivalry, between China and Russia and the possibilities of a change in US policy after an election, or indeed a modulation or variation in it beforehand. As Gerard Baker observed in the London *Times* on July 13, 2023: "As their own relative economic and strategic power has waned in the 21st century, fewer Americans see why they should continue to bear a burden of global leadership that seems like the legacy of a different era of geopolitics." Indeed, on July 13, President Biden faced questioning in Helsinki about the constancy of US policy. One journalist asked: "What actions will you take to assure Finland that the US will remain a reliable NATO partner for decades to come?" Sauli Niinisto, the Finnish president, was asked in the same press conference if he was "worried that the political instability in the US will cause issues in the alliance in the future." Biden had raised doubts by pointing out: "No one can guarantee the future. But this is the best bet anyone can make."

Indeed, about the 2022 midterms and then with reference to a possible Trump victory, concerns voiced in 2022–24 by European and Japanese commentators were not only an expression of anxiety about US consistency and purpose but also, at least implicitly, a critique of geopolitics as a description of what is, as opposed to a rhetoric of what ought to be. The idea of a European Union foreign policy and thus geopolitics very much appeared to be a case of the latter.

Xi Jinping and Vladimir Putin share an existential challenge to geopolitical assumptions based on a rules-based system in which, despite criticisms of them, Western values, national independence, human rights, and democratic practices are all linked, at least as desirable factors. The degree to which this ideological affinity trumps elements in which China and Russia clash is open to discussion. There is no room for a conclusive statement on the matter, and suggestions to the contrary are foolish. Any emphasis above on the shared values of Xi Jinping and Vladimir Putin underline the extent to which geography is scarcely destiny but instead refracted through a multivalent situation.

As a separate point, the idea of a Eurasian geopolitical bloc dominated by authoritarian states becomes more complex under scrutiny, for China, which is definitely authoritarian, centers its power on areas in or near the coastal littoral. As a result, it can be presented as part of a "Rimland" seeking, on a long-standing pattern, to dominate the interior and notably making efforts to do so in Tibet and Xinjiang. Yet again, this underlines the flexibility, indeed porosity, of the terms employed. They are, however, well established. Thus, Xi Jinping, who visited Papua New Guinea when it hosted the 2018 Asia-Pacific Economic Co-operation conference, told James Marape, the prime minister: "China stays committed to equal treatment, mutual respect, win-win co-operation, openness and inclusiveness, without targeting any third party. It has no interest in geopolitical rivalry."

This is an instance of the use of the term *geopolitical* as describing an undesirable practice, in this case rivalry. There is an echo back to the process by which revolutionary regimes, for example, those of the French (1789) and Russian (1917) revolutionaries, were apt to reject the supposed goals, practices, and language of the prerevolutionary governments in international relations. However, typecasting the rhetoric does not mean that the new regimes did not soon follow similar goals and practices, even if the language changed. Moreover, deploring geopolitics, a process also seen after World War II in reaction, notably in the United States, to Karl Ernst Haushofer and the Nazi use of geopolitical ideas,[7] did not prevent its widespread employment by many commentators as a shorthand for all geographical relations with politics.

Alongside the idea of a geopolitical bloc, much can be made about the disparities in population terms east of the Urals, and this can be presented as a geopolitical vulnerability for Russia. The Russian annexation of Chinese territory in 1858–60 in the Amur Valley and the Russian Far East can be seen as a geopolitical grievance that, like most, has a historical origin. Clashing economic interests over the exploitation of Russian resources, especially in Siberia, can be seen as a grievance in the making.

All of these factors provided the potential for playing on Russian anger or concern toward China and for Russia holding a position of choice between the United States and China. The invasion of Ukraine lost Russia that possible geopolitical resource/reserve. Yet, however much this might seem implausible at present, notably from the perspective of an Eastern Europe angry and fearful about Russia, there is the chance of a change.

There is a good historical example. In 1950–53, Chinese forces fought the United States in Korea, and in 1962 the US deployed units to threaten China when it attacked India. Yet, a decade later, the two powers began an alignment. It is easier for authoritarian powers to make such changes, as shown by the 1939–41 German-Soviet alliance. In turn, the Japanese attack on the United States led the latter and the Soviet Union to be on the same side in 1941–45.

Such a process might be spurred by future US governments more concerned about China and happy to delegate regional relations with Russia to Europe, while themselves seeking to weaken China by pursuing better relations with Russia. This approach does not necessarily augur well for relations between the United States and Europe's Russian neighbors, notably those that have been most determined to support Ukraine, a group that also includes Britain. Europe also will be challenged by large-scale immigration.

The US-China-Russia relationships dominate attention at present, but that leaves in the shadows the geopolitical concerns of most states. Moreover, a failure to engage with the latter can help ensure that there is an inability to understand why particular responses are adopted to the great power rivalries. The rivalries of "lesser" states, indeed, are more complex because they also have to consider their response to the major states. The degree to which geography plays a role here is pushed to the fore by the issue of propinquity, as that poses the issue of border instability. The range of weapons, however, as with Iran and Israel, can make propinquity far more extensive than the bordering territory that attracted prime attention in the past.[8]

From this perspective, geopolitics has become truly global, just as geoeconomics has with the ready ability to move money. The need for a new language to conceptualize a geopolitics of such a range is readily apparent. In contrast, it is at the subnational scale where such weaponry is absent or less significant that geopolitics as often understood may be more valuable. In particular, any emphasis on ethnic rivalry as in Congo or South Sudan and on foreign intervention across borders may well mean that issues of location are of particular significance.[9] Again there is the question of how best to reconcile the subnational and the global and what both mean in the context of a modern world that displays a type of hybrid sovereignty.[10] Looking to the future, it is likely that countries will move away from the standard list of geopolitical topics. The challenge for geopolitical conceptualization and application, however, will still include a struggle over meaning and application.

NOTES

PREFACE

1. *Hansard, House of Commons Debates*, March 15, 1883, vol. 277, column 617.

2. *Hansard, House of Commons Debates*, May 7, 1883, vol. 279, columns 125–26.

3. Colin Flint, *Geopolitical Constructs: The Mulberry Harbours, World War Two, and the Making of a Militarized Transatlantic* (Lanham, MD, 2016).

4. William Martel, *Grand Strategy in Theory and Practice* (New York, 2015); Lukas Milevski, *The Evolution of Modern Grand Strategic Thought* (Oxford, 2016); Antulio Echevarria, "Strategic Culture Is Not a Silver Bullet," *Naval War College Review* 70 (2017): 121–24; John Bew, *Realpolitik: A History* (Oxford, 2015); Jeremy Black and Harald Kleinschmidt, "Schroeder Reconsidered or the Limitations of the Systems Approach," *Diplomacy and Statecraft* 11 (2000): 257–70.

5. Sally Paine, *The Japanese Empire: Grand Strategy from the Meiji Restoration to the Pacific War* (Cambridge, 2017).

6. *Times*, July 19, 2023.

7. Zac Cope, editor of the *Handbook*, to Black, July 23, 2023, email.

8. George Soros, "A Partnership with China to Avoid World War," *New York Review of Books*, August 12, 2015, 4.

9. Nicholas Lambert, *The War Lords and the Gallipoli Disaster: How Globalized Trade Led Britain to Its Worst Defeat of the Frist World War* (Oxford, 2021).

10. Nicholas Smith, *Colonial Chaos in the Southern Red Sea: A History of Violence from 1830 to the Twentieth Century* (Cambridge, 2021).

11. Ronald St. John, *Bolivia: Geopolitics of a Landlocked State* (New York, 2021). See, more generally, Tom Long, *A Small State's Guide to Influence in World Politics* (Oxford, 2022).

1. LIBERAL UNIONIST GEOPOLITICS
AND MACKINDER

1. John Hendrickson, *Crisis in the Mediterranean: Naval Competition and Great Power Politics, 1904–1914* (Annapolis, MD, 2014).

2. Holger Herwig, *The Demon of Geopolitics: How Karl Haushofer "Educated" Hitler and Hess* (Lanham, MD, 2016).

3. Jonathan Smele, *The Russian Civil Wars, 1916–1926: Ten Years that Shook the World* (Oxford, 2015).

4. Sarah Lefanu, *Something of Themselves: Kipling, Kingsley, Conan Doyle, and the Anglo-Boer War* (Oxford, 2020); Pascal Venier, "The Geographical Pivot of History and Early Twentieth Century Geopolitical Culture," *Geographical Journal* 170 (2004): 330–36; Duncan Bell, *The Idea of Greater Britain: Empire and the Future of World Order, 1860–1900* (Princeton, NJ, 2007), and *Reordering the World: Essays on Liberalism and Empire* (Princeton, NJ, 2016); John Mitcham, *Race and Imperial Defense in the British World, 1870–1914* (Cambridge, 2016).

5. Benjamin Cooling, *Gray Steel and Blue Water Navy: The Formative Years of America's Military-Industrial Complex, 1881–1917* (Hamden, CT, 1979); Mark Shulman, *Navalism and the Emergence of American Sea Power, 1882–1893* (Annapolis, MD, 1995).

6. Arne Røksund, *The Jeune École: The Strategy of the Weak* (Leiden, 2007).

7. Jesse Tumblin, *The Quest for Security: Sovereignty, Race, and the Defense of the British Empire, 1898–1931* (Cambridge, 2019).

8. Richard Toye, *Churchill's Empire: The World that Made Him and the World He Made* (Oxford, 2010).

9. Suzanne Kuss, *German Colonial Wars and the Context of Military Violence* (Cambridge, MA, 2017).

10. Donald Schurman, *Imperial Defence, 1868–1887* (London, 2000).

11. Andrew Lambert, *Seapower States: Maritime Culture, Continental Empires, and the Conflict that Made the Modern World* (New Haven, CT, 2018).

12. J. Lee Thompson, *Forgotten Patriot: A Life of Alfred, Viscount Milner of St James's and Cape Town, 1854–1925* (Madison, NJ, 2007).

13. Iain Smith, *The Origins of the South African War, 1899–1902* (Harlow, 1996).

14. Bruce Vandervort, *To the Fourth Shore: Italy's War for Libya, 1911–1912* (Rome, 2012).

15. H. J. Mackinder, "The Geographical Pivot of History," *Geographical Journal* 23 (1904): 421–37.

16. Tyler Dennett, "Mahan's 'The Problem of Asia,'" *Foreign Affairs* 13 (1935): 464.

17. Mackinder, "Geographical Pivot of History," 434.

18. Brian Blouet, "The Political Career of Sir Halford Mackinder," *Political Geography Quarterly* 6 (1987): 355–67; Torbjorn Knutsen, "Halford J. Mackinder, Geopolitics and the Heartland Thesis," *International History Review* 36 (2014): 835–57; Louis Halewood, "'Peace throughout the Oceans and Seas of the World': British Maritime Strategic Thought and World Order, 1892–1919," *Historical Research* 94 (2021): 554–77. For criticism of Mackinder as a supporter of empire, Gerry Kearns, "Geography, Geopolitics and Empire," *Transactions of the Institute of British Geographers*, n.s., 35 (2010): 187–203.

19. *Hansard*, House of Lords, June 11, 1877, 3rd ser., vol. 234, col. 1565.

20. Kevin McCranie, *Mahan, Corbett, and the Foundations of Naval Strategic Thought* (Annapolis, MD, 2021).

21. Jack Levy and John Vasquez, eds., *The Outbreak of the First World War: Structure, Politics and Decision-Making* (Cambridge, 2014).

2. FROM WORLD WAR I TO ITS
SEQUEL, 1914–39

1. David Hamlin, *Germany's Empire in the East: Germans and Romania in an Era of Globalization and Total War* (Cambridge, 2017).

2. John Ferris, "The Symbol and Substance of Seapower: Britain, the United States and the One-Power Standard, 1919–1921," in *Anglo-American Relations in the 1920s: The Struggle for Supremacy*, ed. Brian McKercher (Edmonton, 1990), 55–80.

3. Pierpaolo Barbieri, *Hitler's Shadow Empire: Nazi Economics and the Spanish Civil War* (Cambridge, MA, 2017).

4. Robin Higham, *Britain's Imperial Air Routes, 1918–1939* (Hamden, CT, 1960); Robert McCormack, "Imperialism, Air Transport and Colonial Development: Kenya 1920–1946," *Journal of Imperial and Commonwealth History* 17 (1989): 374–95.

5. Kings College London, Liddell Hart Library, Montgomery-Massingberd Papers, vol. 10/6.

6. The Defence Requirements Sub-Committee, Annual Review, October 12, 1933, London, National Archives, Cabinet Papers 24/244, folio 136.

7. William Johnsen, *The Origins of the Grand Alliance: Anglo-American Military Collaboration from the Panay Incident to Pearl Harbor* (Lexington, KY, 2016).

8. Viscount Maugham, *The Truth about the Munich Crisis* (London, 1944), 57–58.

3. US APPROACHES TO GLOBAL STRUGGLE

1. John Thompson, *A Sense of Power: The Roots of America's Global Role* (Ithaca, NY, 2015).

2. William Still, *Crisis at Sea: The United States Navy in European Waters, 1917–1918* (Gainesville, FL, 2006).

3. Beverly Gage, *G-Man: J. Edgar Hoover and the Making of the American Century* (New York, 2023).

4. Adam McKeown, "Global Migration, 1846–1940," *Journal of World History* 15 (2004): 155–89, esp. 172–75.

5. Karl Ittmann, *A Problem of Great Importance: Population, Race and Power in the British Empire, 1918–1973* (Oakland, 2013).

6. Ben Shepherd, *Hitler's Soldiers: The German Army in the Third Reich* (New Haven, CT, 2016).

7. Peter Fritzsche, *An Iron Wind: Europe under Hitler* (New York, 2016).

8. Benjamin Martin, *The Neo-Fascist New Order for European Culture* (Cambridge, MA, 2016).

9. Jeremy Yellen, *The Greater East Asia Co-Prosperity Sphere: When Total Empire Met Total War* (Berlin, 2018); Ethan Mark, *Japan's Occupation of Java in the Second World War: A Transnational History* (London, 2018).

10. Grant Harward, *Romania's Holy War: Soldiers, Motivation, and the Holocaust* (Ithaca, NY, 2021).

11. Marc Milner, "The Atlantic War, 1939–1945: The Case for a New Paradigm," *Global War Studies* 14 (2017): 45–60.

12. Evan Wilson and Ruth Schapiro, "German Perspectives on the U-Boat War, 1939–1941," *Journal of Military History* 85 (2021): 369–98.

13. Anand Toprani, *Oil and the Great Powers: Britain and Germany, 1914–1945* (Oxford, 2019).

14. Cunningham to Sir Dudley Pound, First Lord of the Admiralty, May 28, 1941, London, British Library, Department of Manuscripts, Additional Manuscripts, vol. 52567, folio 117.

4. THE GLOBAL WORLD WAR II

1. Klaus Schmider, *Hitler's Fatal Miscalculation: Why Germany Declared War on the United States* (Cambridge, 2021).

2. Peter John Brobst, "'Icarian Geography': Air Power, Closed Space, and British Decolonisation," *Geopolitics* 9 (2004): 426–39.

3. Jennifer L. Van Vleck, "The 'Logic of the Air': Aviation and the Globalism of the 'American Century,'" *New Global Studies* 1 (2007): 23; Or Rosenboim, "Geopolitics and Empires: Visions of Regional World Order in the 1940s," *Modern Intellectual History* 12 (2015): 353–81.

4. London, British Library, Department of Manuscripts, Additional Manuscripts, vol. 74806.

5. British Library, Map Library, maps 197.h.1.

6. British Library, Map Library, maps 197.h.1.

7. Tami Biddle, "On the Crest of Fear: V-Weapons, the Battle of the Bulge, and the Last Stages of World War II in Europe," *Journal of Military History* 83 (2019): 157–94.

8. Layton to First Sea Lord, September 13, Lord Louis Mountbatten to Layton, September 15, 1944, London, British Library, Department of Manuscripts, Additional Manuscripts, volume 74796.

9. Alexander Hill, *The Great Patriotic War of the Soviet Union, 1941–45: A Documentary Reader* (Abingdon, UK, 2009), 172; and Alexander Hill, "British Lend-Lease Tanks and the Battle of Moscow, November–December 1941—Revisited," *Journal of Slavic Military Studies* 22 (2009): 574–87.

10. Waldo Heinrichs and Marc Gallicchio, *Implacable Foes: War in the Pacific 1944–1945* (New York, 1945).

11. Jonathan Brunstedt, *The Soviet Myth of World War II: Patriotic Memory and the Russian Question in the USSR* (Cambridge, 2021).

12. Rana Mitter, *China's Good War: How World War II Is Shaping a New Nationalism* (Cambridge, MA, 2020).

13. D. M. Giangreco, *Hell to Pay: Operation DOWNFALL and the Invasion of Japan, 1945–1947* (Annapolis, MD, 2017).

5. THE LIBERAL INTERNATIONALISM
OF COLD WAR US GEOPOLITICS

1. Peter John Brobst, *The Future of the Great Game: Sir Olaf Caroe, India's Independence and the Defense of Asia* (Akron, OH, 2005), 48, 79–83, 95–98.

2. Nicolas Spykman, *The Geography of the Peace*, ed. Helen Nicholl (New York, 1944), 25, 57.

3. Seth Cropsey, "Naval Considerations in the Russo-Ukrainian War," *Naval War College Review* 75 (2022): 30.

4. Michael Neiberg, *Potsdam: The End of World War II and the Remaking of Europe* (New York, 2015); Alan Sharp, *Versailles 1919: A Centennial Perspective* (Chicago, 2018).

5. London, National Archives, Foreign Office Papers, 371/56753, folio 26.

6. Steve Call, *Selling Air Power: Military Aviation and American Popular Culture after World War II* (College Station, TX, 2009).

7. Anthony Wells, *A Tale of Two Navies: Geopolitics, Technology, and Strategy in the United States Navy and the Royal Navy, 1960–2015* (Annapolis, MD, 2017).

8. Alessio Palatano, *Post-War Japan as a Sea Power: Imperial Legacy, Wartime Experience, and the Making of a Navy* (London, 2015).

9. William Rust, *Eisenhower and Cambodia: Diplomacy, Covert Action, and the Origins of the Second Indochina War* (Lexington, KY, 2016).

10. Peter Hahn, "Securing the Middle East: The Eisenhower Doctrine of 1957," *Presidential Studies Quarterly* 36, no. 1 (2006): 38–47.

11. Masuda Hajimu, *Cold War Crucible: The Korean Conflict and the Postwar World* (Cambridge, MA, 2015).

12. Jonathan House, *A Military History of the Cold War, 1962–1991* (Norman, OK, 2020).

13. Trevor Albertson, *Winning Armageddon: Curtis LeMay and Strategic Air Command, 1948–1957* (Annapolis, MD, 2019).

14. Joshua-John Seah, "Singapore, Hong Kong, and the Royal Navy's War in Korea, c. 1950–1953," *Journal of Military History* 83 (2019): 1213–34.

15. Mark Gjessing, *Anglo-Australian Naval Relations, 1945–1975: A More Independent Service* (Basingstoke, UK, 2018).

16. Kosal Path, *Vietnam's Strategic Thinking during the Third Indochina War* (Madison, WI, 2020).

17. William Pickett, "The Eisenhower Solarium Notes," *Society for Historians of American Foreign Relations Newsletter* 16

(June 1985): 1–10; Gregory Mitrovich, *Undermining the Kremlin: America's Strategy to Subvert the Soviet Bloc, 1947–1956* (Ithaca, NY, 2000).

18. Pickett, "The Eisenhower Solarium Notes."

19. Rodric Braithwaite, *Armageddon and Paranoia: The Nuclear Confrontation since 1945* (Oxford, 2018).

20. Bill Yenne, *B-52 Stratofortress* (Minneapolis, 2012).

21. Janet Abbate, *Inventing the Internet* (Cambridge, MA, 1999).

22. John Slessor, *Strategy for the West* (New York, 1954), 34, see also his *The Great Deterrent* (New York, 1957), 127.

23. *Foreign Relations of the United States, 1952–1954, Indochina*, vol. 13, part 1, doc. 716, 1281–82; *Public Papers of the Presidents of the United States: Dwight D. Eisenhower, 1954*, 381–90.

24. Peter Hahn, "Securing the Middle East: The Eisenhower Doctrine of 1957," *Presidential Studies Quarterly* 36 (2006): 38–47.

25. Lawrence Tal, "Britain and the Jordan Crisis of 1958," *Middle Eastern Studies* 31 (1995): 39–57.

26. Edward O'Dowd, *Chinese Military Strategy in the Third Indochina War: The Last Maoist War* (London, 2007); Xiaoming Zhang, *Deng Xiaoping's Long War: The Military Conflict between China and Vietnam, 1979–1991* (Chapel Hill, NC, 2015).

27. Christian Lentz, *Contested Territory: Điện Biên Phủ and the Making of Northwest Vietnam* (New Haven, CT, 2019); Geoffrey Jensen and Matthew Stith, eds., *Beyond the Quagmire: New Interpretations of the Vietnam War* (Denton, TX, 2019).

28. Bradford Dismukes, "The Return of Great-Power Competition: Cold War Lessons about Strategic Antisubmarine Warfare and Defense of Sea Lines of Communication," *Naval War College Review* 73 (2020): 33–57.

29. Thomas Nichols, "Carter and the Soviets: The Origins of the US Return to a Strategy of Confrontation," *Diplomacy and Statecraft* 13, no. 2 (2002): 21–42.

30. Andrew Bacevich, *America's War for the Greater Middle East: A Military History* (New York, 2016).

31. Wells, *Tale of Two Navies.*

6. AN ASCENDANT WORLD ORDER SLIPS
UNDER PRESSURE, 1989–2021

1. M. Taylor Travel, *Active Defense: China's Military Strategy since 1949* (Princeton, NJ, 2019).

2. Donald Stoker, *Why America Loses Wars: Limited War and US Strategy from the Korean War to the Present* (Cambridge, 2019).

3. David Fitzgerald, "Warriors Who Don't Fight: The Post–Cold War United States Army and Debates over Peacekeeping Operations," *Journal of Military History* 85 (2021): 163–90.

4. Pat Procter, *Lessons Unlearned: The U.S. Army's Role in Creating the Forever Wars in Afghanistan and Iraq* (Columbia, MS, 2020).

5. Beth Bailey and Richard Immerman, eds., *Understanding the U.S. Wars in Iraq and Afghanistan* (New York, 2015); Metin Gurcan, *What Went Wrong in Afghanistan? Understanding Counter-Insurgency Efforts in Tribalized Rural and Muslim Environments* (Solihull, UK, 2016).

6. James Kurth, *The American Way of Empire: How America Won a World—but Lost Her Way* (Washington, DC, 2019).

7. Joseph Stieb, *The Regime Change Consensus: Iraq in American Politics, 1990–2003* (Cambridge, 2021).

8. Srinath Raghavan, *Fierce Enigmas: A History of the United States in South Asia* (New York, 2018).

9. Colin Gordon, *Citizen Brown: Race, Democracy, and Inequality in the St. Louis Suburbs* (Chicago, 2019).

10. Aaron Stein, *The US War against ISIS: How America and Its Allies Defeated the Caliphate* (London, 2022).

11. Ido Levy, *Soldiers of End-Times: Assessing the Military Effectiveness of the Islamic State* (Washington, DC, 2021).

12. Tanja Börzel and Vera Hüllen, eds., *Governance Transfer by Regional Organisations* (London, 2015).

13. Max Harris, "Greasing the World's Wheels," *Times Literary Supplement*, July 14, 2023, 9.

14. Mark Leonard, "China Is Ready for a World of Disorder," *Foreign Affairs* 102, no. 4 (July/August 2023): 126–27.

15. Mark Thatcher and Tim Vlandas, *Foreign States in Domestic Markets: Sovereign Wealth Funds and the West* (Oxford, 2021).

16. Martin Daunton, *The Economic Government of the World, 1933–2023* (London, 2023). For an up-to-date account of geopolitics and business, see C. Nestorovic, *Geopolitics and Business. Relevance and Resonance* (Singapore, 2023).

7. THE GEOPOLITICS OF THE PRESENT

1. John Denni, *Coalition of the UnWilling and UnAble: European Realignment and the Future of American Geopolitics* (Ann Arbor, MI, 2021).

2. Steven Wills, *Strategy Shelved: The Collapse of Cold War Naval Strategic Planning* (Annapolis, MD, 2021).

3. "How Did the Russia-Ukraine War Trigger a Global Food Crisis?," *Al Jazeera*, June 18, 2022, https://www.aljazeera.com /economy/2022/6/18/explainer-how-did-russia-ukraine-war -trigger-a-food-crisis.

4. Daniel Yergin, *The New Map: Energy, Climate, and the Clash of Nations* (New York, 2020).

5. Michael Klare, *The Race for What's Left: The Global Struggle for the World's Last Resources* (New York, 2012).

6. Matthew Kroenig, *The Return of Great Power Rivalry: Democracy versus Autocracy from the Ancient World to the U.S. and China* (Oxford, 2020).

7. Brian Fong, "What's Driving the Democratic Recession in Asia?," *International Affairs* 99 (2023): 1273–91.

8. Marianne Kneuer and Thomas Demmelhuber, "Gravity Centres of Authoritarian Rule: A Conceptual Approach," *Democratisation* 23 (2016): 775–96.

9. Sarah Paine, "Centuries of Security: Chinese, Russian and U.S. Continental versus Maritime Approaches," *Journal of Military History* 86 (2022): 813–36. For a similar emphasis, see Paul Kennedy, *Victory at Sea: Naval Power and the Transformation of the Global Order in World War II* (New Haven, CT, 2022).

10. I have benefited from reading Harold Tanner, "American Understandings of Chinese Strategy: A First-Draft Genealogy of the Search for a Chinese Way of War" (unpublished paper).

11. Robin Mukherjee, *Ascending Order: Rising Powers and the Politics of Status in International Relations* (Cambridge, 2022).

12. Thomas Wilkins and Jiye Kim, "Adoption, Accommodation or Opposition? Regional Powers Respond to American-Led Indo-Pacific Strategy," *Pacific Review* 35 (2022): 415–45.

13. Oscar Jonsson, *The Russian Understanding of War: Blurring the Lines between War and Peace* (Washington, DC, 2019).

8. INTO THE FUTURE

1. John Foster, *Capitalism in the Anthropocene: Ecological Ruin or Ecological Revolution* (New York, 2022).

2. Niall Ferguson, "Russia's Farcical Mutiny Is Deadly Serious for China and Iran," Bloomberg, July 1, 2023, https://www.bloomberg.com/opinion/articles/2023-07-02/russia-s-farcical-mutiny-is-deadly-serious-for-iran-china-niall-ferguson.

3. Though see Klaus Dodds, "Geopolitics and the Geographical Imagination of Argentina," in *Geopolitical Traditions*, ed. Klaus Dodds and D. Atkinson (London, 2000), 150–84.

4. Daniel Moore, *Offensive Cyber Operations: Understanding Intangible Warfare* (London, 2022).

5. Joseph Trevithich, The Drive, July 11, 2022, https://www.thedrive.com.

6. Elbridge Colby, *The Strategy of Denial: American Defense in an Age of Great Power Conflict* (New Haven, CT, 2021).

7. Derwent Whittlesey and Hans W. Weigert, "Geopolitics," *Encyclopaedia Britannica* 10 (Chicago, 1963): 182.

8. Ehud Eilam, *Containment in the Middle East* (Lincoln, NE, 2019).

9. Jason Stearns, *The War that Doesn't Say Its Name: Unending Conflict in the Congo* (Princeton, NJ, 2021).

10. Swati Srivastava, *Hybrid Sovereignty in World Politics* (Cambridge, 2022).

INDEX

INDEX

resources: extraction of, 149–50; future geopolitics, 161; Nazi Germany and, 37; population growth and, 124–25; present-day geopolitics, 135–39; rail transport of, 33–34; Ukraine war and, 135–37; wartime access and allocation, 35, 49; WWI geopolitics, 33–34, 35

responsible government, 17–18

revanchism, 54, 104, 114

Revenge of Geography: What the Map Tells Us about Coming Conflicts and the Battle against Fate, The (Kaplan), xii–xiii

revisionism, 74

revolutionary regimes, 161

revolution in military affairs (RMA), 109

Rhein-Main Air Base, 82

rhetoric: Cold War era, 81; future scenarios, 151–52, 160, 161; geopolitics and, x, xi–xii, xiv; present day, 144; pre-WWI era, 6; WWII era, 41, 50

Rieber, Alfred, 111

rimland theory: Cold War geopolitics, 72; future geopolitics, 153–54; interwar-period geopolitics, 40; modern-era geopolitics, 117, 120; present-day geopolitics, 73; Vietnam War geopolitics, 90–91

Rio Tinto, 120

rivalry: autocracies vs. democracies, 142; ethnic, 163; future geopolitics, 159, 162–63; geopolitics and, xvii, 125, 126–27; great powers, 110, 132, 162–63; present-day geopolitics, 142, 148

River War: An Historical Account of the Reconquest of the Soudan, The (Churchill), 13–14

RMA (revolution in military affairs), 109

roads, 63, 68, 82. *See also* land routes

Robert, 3rd Marquess of Salisbury, 20, 23

Roberts, Frank, 75–76

robots, 158

rocketry, 149, 158

rogue states, 113, 126

rollback strategy, 35, 84, 89

Romania, 33, 55, 118

Rome, 10

Roosevelt, Franklin Delano, 56, 59

Roosevelt, Theodore "Teddy," 6

routes. *See* land routes; rail systems; sea routes; transportation routes

Royal Geographical Society, 21

Royal Titles Act, 17

Rumsfeld, Donald, 109

Russia: Afghanistan and, 146; air bases, 117–18; air power, 118; allies of (modern era), 115–16; Britain and, ix, 4, 7, 14–15, 20, 39, 75, 99; China and (future geopolitics), 158, 160, 161–62; China and (modern era), 116, 122; China and (present day), 140, 146, 159; China and (pre-WWI), 1, 24–26, 46, 161; Civil War, 4; energy production, 138; expansionism and imperialism of, 10, 22–26, 159; Far East and, 26, 161; France and, 77, 143; future geopolitics, 149–63; Germany and, 31, 33, 34–35, 96;

198

JEREMY BLACK is a preeminent historian and author of numerous books, including *A Brief History of History, Tank Warfare,* and *Charting the Past: The Historical Worlds of Eighteenth-Century England.* He is Emeritus Professor of History at the University of Exeter and a Senior Fellow both of the British Foreign Policy Group and of the Foreign Policy Research Institute. Black is a recipient of the Samuel Eliot Morison Prize from the Society for Military History. Follow Black on his website, jeremyblackhistorian.wordpress.com.

For Indiana University Press

Dan Crissman, Trade and Regional
    Acquisitions Editor
Anna Francis, Assistant Acquisitions Editor
Anna Garnai, Editorial Assistant
Brenna Hosman, Production Coordinator
Katie Huggins, Production Manager
Darja Malcolm-Clarke, Project Manager/Editor
Dan Pyle, Online Publishing Manager
Michael Regoli, Director of Publishing Operations
Jennifer Witzke, Senior Artist and Book Designer